Using Social Media to
Build Library Communities

LIBRARY INFORMATION TECHNOLOGY ASSOCIATION (LITA) GUIDES

Marta Mestrovic Deyrup, Ph.D.
Acquisitions Editor, Library Information and Technology Association, a division of the American Library Association

The Library Information Technology Association (LITA) Guides provide information and guidance on topics related to cutting-edge technology for library and IT specialists.

Written by top professionals in the field of technology, the guides are sought after by librarians wishing to learn a new skill or to become current in today's best practices.

Each book in the series has been overseen editorially since conception by LITA and reviewed by LITA members with special expertise in the specialty area of the book.

Established in 1966, LITA is the division of the American Library Association (ALA) that provides its members and the library and information science community as a whole with a forum for discussion, an environment for learning, and a program for actions on the design, development, and implementation of automated and technological systems in the library and information science field.

Approximately 25 LITA Guides were published by Neal-Schuman and ALA between 2007 and 2015. Rowman & Littlefield took over publication of the series beginning in late 2015. Books in the series published by Rowman & Littlefield are:

Digitizing Flat Media: Principles and Practices
The Librarian's Introduction to Programming Languages
Library Service Design: A LITA Guide to Holistic Assessment, Insight, and Improvement
Data Visualization: A Guide to Visual Storytelling for Librarians
Mobile Technologies in Libraries: A LITA Guide
Innovative LibGuides Applications
Integrating LibGuides into Library Websites
Protecting Patron Privacy: A LITA Guide
The LITA Leadership Guide: The Librarian as Entrepreneur, Leader, and Technologist
Using Social Media to Build Library Communities: A LITA Guide

Using Social Media to Build Library Communities

A LITA Guide

Edited by
Scott W. H. Young
Doralyn Rossmann

ROWMAN & LITTLEFIELD
Lanham • Boulder • New York • London

Published by Rowman & Littlefield
A wholly owned subsidiary of The Rowman & Littlefield Publishing Group, Inc.
4501 Forbes Boulevard, Suite 200, Lanham, Maryland 20706
www.rowman.com

Unit A, Whitacre Mews, 26-34 Stannary Street, London SE11 4AB

British Library Cataloguing in Publication Information Available

Library of Congress Cataloging-in-Publication Data Available

ISBN 978-1-4422-7050-3 (hardback : alk. paper) | ISBN 978-1-4422-7051-0 (pbk. : alk. paper) | ISBN 978-1-4422-7052-7 (electronic)

∞™ The paper used in this publication meets the minimum requirements of American National Standard for Information Sciences—Permanence of Paper for Printed Library Materials, ANSI/NISO Z39.48-1992.

Printed in the United States of America

Contents

Figures

Tables

Acknowledgments

Scott W. H. Young and Doralyn Rossmann wish to thank their colleagues at Montana State University Library and across the profession who provide countless ideas and endless inspiration. Most especially, this book simply would not have been possible without the work and insight of the contributing authors. Our many, many thanks to Lisa, Laura, Andrew, Jessica, Rebecca, Dana, Angel, Patricia, Chris, Joanna, Stony, Katie, Jarrett, and April.

Lisa Bunker would like to acknowledge Jen Maney, Justine Hernandez, Jessica Pryde, Karen Elson Anderson, Lupita Chavez, and Lori Thayer. Chris Chan and Joanna Hare would like to thank the senior management of their respective libraries for their support of this project. April Hathcock offers heartfelt thanks to all those who make up her critical community on Twitter and beyond. You challenge and encourage her in so many ways and she is grateful. Dana Knott would like to thank Columbus State Community College, the Columbus State Library, and, in particular, outreach and engagement librarian Julie Zaveloff for her expertise and assistance.

Preface

PURPOSE

Libraries build communities. By fostering idea exchange and knowledge building, libraries help shape and sustain communities at universities, cities, small towns, online venues, and every other place where a library is found. Strong communities of all kinds are underpinned by common characteristics—unity, shared purpose, and shared values. In these strong communities, the library can be an active participant in expressing communal values, thereby cultivating a collective power among librarians and library users alike. As both a place and as a service, the library then functions as a dynamic social force for bringing real people together and effecting real change, ultimately for the benefit of its diverse communities.

From this context, *Using Social Media to Build Library Communities: A LITA Guide* represents a community-building action manual for practitioners across the profession. By bringing together an array of perspectives to explore community building through social media, *Using Social Media to Build Communities: A LITA Guide* can serve as the go-to resource for professionals who want to take social media beyond marketing and promotion to build an inclusive and engaged community of library users.

Libraries often focus their social media efforts on marketing library services and events. Consequently, many books, articles, and blog posts in the library literature characterize marketing and outreach as the primary function of social media. From this perspective, social media takes on a product-focused, one-way, broadcast-oriented style of communication. While promotion is an important aspect of social media and indeed necessary for libraries in general, we do not believe this to be the main purpose of social media. Rather, we see social media as a tool for conversation, community, and social good. As trusted members of our communities, libraries can approach social media with a people-focused, interactive, dialogue-oriented communication that aims to build a sense of connection and unity through shared purpose and shared values.

Using Social Media to Build Library Communities: A LITA Guide can help you build your community. The contributors to this volume have built communities of users in public libraries, academic libraries, and community college libraries. They have built communities of fellow social media practitioners, educators, and information professionals. And they have built communities and collections where social justice and critical dialogue are central driving forces. In assembling such experience and expertise, this book aims to generate motivation and momentum toward a practice of social media that is focused primarily on building community relationships through personal connection.

STRUCTURE

The chapters of *Using Social Media to Build Library Communities: A LITA Guide* are organized into three thematic parts.

Part I, "Building Communities of Library Users," opens with a suite of case studies demonstrating real-world community-building practices in a variety of library settings: public library (chapter 1), academic library (chapter 2), community college library (chapter 3), and health-sciences library (chapter 4). Chapter 1 also features overviews of today's leading social media platforms and offers guidance for finding a voice on social media that can be applied in any library context. Taken together, these chapters will provide a practical getting-started road map that can be adapted for your local environment. Part I is rounded out by a chapter that details the strategies and impacts of advertising on Facebook (chapter 5), which can help you continue to build your community using the ad-placement mechanisms of Facebook.

Part II, "Building Communities of Library Professionals," focuses on the methods for building communities of fellow practitioners. Finding and connecting with other like-minded professionals is essential for learning and growing as a social media practitioner. Building communities of practice (chapter 6) and building a personal learning network (chapter 7) are valuable approaches for sharing ideas and building expertise in social media.

Part III, "Transforming Community into Action—Social Media and Social Justice," highlights the capacity for social media to effect social good and social justice. Where archival practice intersects with social media practice (chapter 8), new voices can be preserved and amplified. For information professionals seeking to engage critically with the profession through the lens of social justice (chapter 9), social media can provide the connection points and direction for challenging ourselves and our profession to learn and grow together toward a more equal and inclusive future.

AUDIENCE

This book is intended for information professionals who want to use social media to build and sustain dynamic library communities. The expertise level of this book is situated somewhere between introductory and intermediate, ideal for those getting started with social media and for those looking to deepen and extend community connection. In essence, *Using Social Media to Build Library Communities: A LITA Guide* demonstrates that an energetic and committed community exists to help and guide fellow community builders. Use this book to guide your own social media practice toward community building.

CONTINUING THE CONVERSATION

To build a community of practice around this book and its readers, we encourage you to share your perspectives and experiences through social media by using the hashtag #SocialMediaLITAguide.

I

BUILDING COMMUNITIES OF LIBRARY USERS

1

Picking a Platform and Finding a Voice

Lisa Bunker

OVERVIEW

Because of social media, we're beginning to learn how to be a living, breathing library online. The tools may be digital, but have no doubt that the people you can reach and interact with are real. This chapter has worksheets and information that will help you think strategically about social media as a part of your outward-facing presence and acquaint you with the strengths and challenges of the different platforms. Let's first look at what can be done when community, platform, message, and voice are aligned.

A CASE STUDY IN GROWING COMMUNITY ONLINE

Back in 2011, Pima County Public Library librarian Justine Hernandez didn't just want the library to create a system for lending seeds; she wanted to add the library's voice to southern Arizona's emerging heritage food and sustenance gardening movements. As she put it, "Public libraries are our society's commons whose province is the equitable and accessible dissemination of information. And seeds are information: they're history, culture, journey, ingenuity, nourishment, possibility, people, story."[1]

Months before its January 2012 launch, Justine asked me to set up a Facebook page for the seed library.[2] There was real necessity. Despite strong internal commitment from the top on down here at Pima County, we learned there would be no official publicity. Our public information officer was leaving for another job and unable to make anything for the launch—no poster, no press release, no phone calls to reporters. We had to work with what we could make for ourselves, and that included a Facebook page.[3]

Luckily we had other things working for us: Justine's personal outreach to community gardens, gardening clubs, and farmer's markets; her personal networking on Facebook; intense interest from local food and community bloggers; and, eventually, interest from traditional media outlets like the newspaper and TV news. Justine wasn't even a gardener at the time, but she was determined to explore and use what she had.

So the "Seed Library of Pima County Public Library" Facebook page was launched. Justine may have been a freshly trained newbie, but very quickly I was learning from her about Facebook's power for programming on the fly and for networking with like-minded organizations, and about where you can go when you really know your audience. She had used hidden skills too: luscious you-are-there photography, a love of corny puns, and an informal writing style that swept its readers along in infectious enthusiasm for trying something new.

On Facebook, Justine took her readers with her as she attended the local seed-saving school, showcased local resources, and invited everyone to help with the enormous task of seed sorting by calling the pop-up events "hootenannys" and "pachangas." She also took us with her as she explored local farmers' markets and heritage gardens, and she brought us behind the scenes where library staff were developing the cataloging system and searching for vintage card catalogs to house the seeds.

Today, with no money for advertising, the page's following is more than twenty-seven-hundred strong and consistently has some of the highest engagement of all of our twenty-five Facebook accounts.

In February 2017, the seed library celebrated five years of seed lending. It has been a resounding success. Seed circulation went from sixty-four-hundred-plus packets in 2012 to twenty-six-thousand-plus packets in 2015. An average of 28 percent of the seeds we now loan were ones "returned" to us by our local gardeners.

What about impact? Yes, Justine and her team[4] met all their goals, but they also unknowingly organized advocates for the library that didn't exist before. In 2013, conservative members of our state legislature wrote a bill that would hurt libraries across the state; it would be especially disastrous for our county and the library system. In response to the bill, the supporters of the seed library did something I had never seen before on our social media.[5]

It is official county policy to strictly limit what its staff can do to officially advocate for our departments, even when it is in our clear interest. When the news of the bill hit, we were told to step back and let unaffiliated organizations and community members respond, without prompting from staff. I was fascinated to watch seed library users organize themselves and offer each other unprompted support for letter writing, phone calling, strategy, and accurate talking points. My state senator told me legislators were surprised by the level of community opposition. The bill never made it out of committee, and I'm certain that passion for the seed library initiative was part of the reason people stepped up.

The "seedy" community, as Justine sometimes calls them, has supported the library in other ways. In 2015, the Pima County Public Library was chosen as the location for the First International Seed Library Forum,[6] and the planners asked Justine to be one of the keynote speakers. Tucson recently became the first American city to become an official UNESCO "City of Gastronomy,"[7] and Tucson's embrace of our public seed library was listed as one of the factors.

Here, I believe, are the lessons learned for social media writers and anyone who wants to create impactful programming:

1. Know your community. Visit, listen, learn, and be helpful. Consider all the ways that "helpfulness" can be translated into content your readers will value.
2. Add to that a communication channel they are already using and make it as helpful, warm, and friendly as your library's in-person presence.
3. Social media combined with coordinated personal contact is much more powerful than social media outreach alone.
4. Take chances, and use the full range of the platform's capabilities to see what works best for your specific library or collection.

This project remains a successful example of library social media because community, platform, message, and voice were all aligned.

You can also think about the seed library's success as a map.

PICKING A PLATFORM

Why Are You on Social Media, and What Will You Say?

Why are you on social media? The answer should be more specific than "We need to be there" or "The new director insists" or "More people need to know about our events." Here are some typical reasons why libraries might decide to be on social media:

- We want more people to visit our website and catalog.
- We want to build awareness, loyalty, and trust with our customers.
- We have a growing number of customers who never visit our buildings. They are online, and we want to provide customer service to them too.
- We frequently have news we need to get out quickly.
- We're an archive or special collection with hidden wonders.
- We know our customers value real-time news and updates.
- We believe the library has a role to play in modeling good citizenship on social media and in helping people assess the accuracy of what they read online.
- We need a responsive showcase that we control for our library's strengths: our staff, the vibrancy of what our community brings to our spaces every day, our

strong partnerships with other community organizations, and how we create good news every day.

- We need to reach our university's students and show them how the library can help with projects.
- We have customers outside our immediate area; we want to entice them back for another visit.
- We have amazing programs that the public never hears about because we haven't been able to tell our own story before—in our own voice—in the media.
- We know that local media are on social media too, and we want another way to pique their interest in what we're doing.

The messages above are intended as examples and may only be partially useful for your library. There is excellent assistance in developing your own key messages on the American Library Association website. Recent books on branding will also be helpful.[8]

- Developing and Implementing a Simple Media/Communications Plan: www. ala.org/advocacy/advleg/publicawareness/campaign@yourlibrary/prtools/hand book/media-plan
- Key Messages: www.ala.org/advocacy/advleg/publicawareness/campaign@your library/aboutyourlibrary/keymessages

Who Is Your Community?

Who do you need to reach? To whom are you talking? Know why you're there, but also consider to whom you expect to be talking. Think about writing a letter to a stranger. Then think about writing a letter to someone you know. Everything is easier when you have an audience (or audiences) in mind as you write.

Is it Community Organizer Daniel? Brian from the nearby halfway house? Retired Art Professor Barbara? Thania the Harry Potter Fan? Chris the Overwhelmed Freshman? Influential Ms. Big? Krystal the Stressed-Out Young Parent? Lashawn the History Nerd? Gabe the Job Hunter? Felicia the Entrepreneur, who just discovered the library's business center? Gwen who lives on a remote ranch? Or Stan the Books by Mail Customer?

Write to a specific, not a general, audience, and what you post will be more interesting to read.

Community-Building Exercises: Envision Your Audience

Start with three very specific audiences you hope to reach through social media.

Write your answers below. Your audience may be customers, or it may be adjacent groups like local news media and library governance and stakeholders.

Examples: parents with children ages one to nine who want to enrich their child's learning at school. Or people who are striving to improve their chances of finding a better-paying job. Or people who love the library but haven't visited in a while. Or people who use our digital resources but don't or can't visit our buildings anymore.

1. _____
2. _____
3. _____

What Are Your Key Messages?

Start by listing key messages in the top row of the table below (see table 1.1 with examples), and then think about how you can adapt them for social media. It will help to go back to the section above where we discussed why your library wants or needs a social media presence.

An example of a key message is

- "We are a place where creative people come for help getting started."
- "You won't believe what you can learn and do at the library."
- "We are a friendly place with very helpful, knowledgeable staff."
- "Our library is the perfect place to study."
- "We help students succeed."
- "We care about our students."
- "We have unique information resources of interest to you."
- "We make your research more discoverable."
- "All are welcome at the library. We don't just welcome diversity; we celebrate it."
- "Our library really understands how to help area businesses."
- "We really 'get' readers and what delights them."
- "Our archive contains authentic history that is very relevant today."
- "We are always looking for new ways to teach literacy."
- "Your library will surprise you."
- "We're helping get our city back to work by teaching job skills and providing expert assistance with the search."
- "We offer powerful ways to learn informally."

If your strategic plan is up to date, your system's stated priorities will be a good place to start. So are your library's aspirations and vision for the future. It may also help to think about the ways that the library is different from similar institutions in your area. What's your library's secret sauce?

Then in the second row of the table, brainstorm five ways you can show how it is happening at the library.

Table 1.1.   Social Media Key Messages

Message "Your library will surprise you."	Message	Message
How can you **show** this on social media with stories, photos, short movies, or graphics?	How can you **show** this on social media with stories, photos, short movies, or graphics?	How can you **show** this on social media with stories, photos, short movies, or graphics?
1. Meet the therapy dogs that will be here during finals. 2. She's borrowing rutabagas from the library. Rutabaga seeds, that is. 3. A funny report on what happened at Adult Storytime last night. 4. Here's a thank-you note from Mr. Sanchez, who borrowed a Wi-Fi hot spot from the library. 5. We're blown away by this video that teens filmed and edited here at the library.		

AUDIENCE, MEDIUM, AND MESSAGE

Consider how a social media presence is different from traditional marketing. With traditional media (newspapers, television, radio), we were used to others making the decisions about what was news, what was important, who spoke for us, and how often we got publicity. Because it was so difficult, the stakes were very high. High value was placed on professional approach, language, and how "newsworthy" a story was.

One side effect of this was that library publicity was very focused on getting the word out for large events, especially ones where attendance was important for success. Programs aimed at more closed audiences, such as early literacy classes for teen parents or support for English learners, were much less visible to people who read the local paper.

Social media is quite different. Libraries finally have the opportunity to decide what the stories are, to use our own authentic voices, and to speak directly to those who are interested in what's happening. We can also build organic community around new initiatives (a seed library, for example) at relatively low cost. These social tools may be digital, but they can help us be more "real" in this age of attention bubbles, distractions, and the growing distrust of traditional marketing messages.

Another change caused by social media is how much easier it is for our visitors and other constituents to complain when they are disappointed in something the library has done (or that they *think* the library has done). For this reason, there are some platforms that one should monitor for comments and reviews, even if you are not going to post. Even after six years of writing for my library, I still get nervous when we are criticized publicly on social media, but I have found it's better to have a difficult conversation earlier, out in the open, rather than later where others might control the forum, such as partisan news. Responding quickly and openly to complaints also showcases your library's great listening skills and empathy for all.[9]

So, yes, you can approach social media the same way you approach traditional news media (only posting big events, lots of marketing messaging, no spontaneity), but your accounts will not reach their full potential and you will be disappointed in your results. Use the exercise above to think in fresh ways about whom you are speaking to on social media and what you have to say.

One final note about audience: there is no social media platform that will help you reach everyone. Even Facebook has its limits. Teens, people with low English skills, new immigrants and refugees, parents working two jobs, and professions with privacy and liability concerns such as lawyers, law enforcement, and doctors are unlikely to use social media at all, much less connect to a library. For the disenfranchised, non-users, and teens, I believe person-to-person contact is still the best way to create and maintain relationships.

Platforms and Communities

What do the various social media services offer for libraries? How is Twitter used compared to Instagram? Which one is a better fit for your library or library system?

Facebook, and to some extent Twitter, try to do it all: text, photos, video, and so on. Facebook has also recently added support for live streaming (à la Snapchat) and strengthened their events system to compete with Meetup and Eventbrite. Reportedly recruiting and job search services are in the works so they will also be in competition with LinkedIn.

The remaining social media platforms all have specific niches, and since the activity is different, the opportunities for creating community differ too. I will address the benefits by the type of community activity, then explore in detail what each major social media service offers.

Image-Focused Communities

Image-focused communities like Instagram are some of the fastest-growing social media platforms right now[10] and offer the power of good pictures to quickly convey not just an event, but also meaning and the emotion behind it. Visual content can include photos, video, and infographics.

Demographics: These services have wide appeal but have been more heavily adopted by women, young people, artists, photographers, illustrators, and celebrities.

The opportunities for libraries, aside from a growing audience, are in the power that images have to quickly convey information, build empathy and awareness, and make your libraries more "real" in the virtual world. The preference is for unposed (but good quality), eye-catching images and visual storytelling.

Examples of image-focused communities: Instagram, Pinterest, and Flickr.

Live-Streaming Image Communities

Live-streaming image communities are centered around raw snippets of life shared through real-time video or photography. For a visit to the movies, a user might film a short snippet for friends as they get ready, another once they arrive, and another afterward with brief commentary on how it went. These videos can be archived, but by default they disappear after twenty-four hours. The appeal is in the seeming authenticity and immediacy of the imagery sent by friends and celebrities.

Demographics: primarily youth and young adults under the age of twenty-four, mostly female.[11] Use by older people is growing quickly, especially now that Facebook and Instagram have added streaming.

For libraries, especially those that serve youth and young adults, these platforms can offer a library a way to become more accessible to students and other young visitors, to speak their visual language.

Examples of live-streaming communities: Snapchat, Facebook Live, Instagram Stories, and Periscope. YouTube also allows live streaming and is reportedly working on an app called YouTube Connect.

IM-Based Communities

The appeal with Instant Messaging (IM) is immediacy and privacy, especially for teens and young adults.[12] People who IM are communicating only with people they know, not the world at large, so these platforms only have benefits for libraries that offer reference assistance and customer service via chat and IM. This is also called "narrowcasting," as opposed to "broadcasting."

Examples of IM-based communities: WhatsApp, WeChat, Viber, and Kik. Snapchat, too, though the "messages" are more visual than textual.

Bulletin Board Communities

Bulletin boards like Reddit unite members of fandoms, hobbies, games, belief systems, and other specialized interests and allow them to subscribe to topical bulletin boards. Reddit is the geek Burning Man of the Internet and a difficult platform for libraries due to its extreme resistance to messaging and anything redditors see as marketer behavior. However, monitoring is also of value for individual library staff, especially the r/Libraries/ subreddit for learning, support, and networking.

Examples of bulletin board communities: Reddit and Digg.

Book-Focused Communities

Book-focused communities unite readers, authors, bloggers, and editors over book reviews and quotes or excerpts. The benefits are primarily personal, although libraries can learn a lot here about the possibilities for creating book-centric community on our own websites.

Here are some of the popular ones:

- *Goodreads*, a large, active community of book lovers, which was purchased by Amazon.com in 2013. Libraries may form groups for book clubs or readers' advisory at no cost, but about 70 percent of the library accounts appear to be inactive in the past twelve months. Look to Salt Lake, Sacramento, and Topeka and Shawnee County Public Libraries for examples of active, successful groups.[13] If your readers are split between Facebook and Goodreads, it is possible to add a Goodreads tab to your library's Facebook page.[14]
- *LibraryThing*, one of the first social media sites for book lovers. It is still one of the best for cataloging a personal collection, but library groups don't seem to have traction. Not to be confused with a related product, LibraryThing for Libraries, which is a paid catalog enhancement service.
- *Litsy* is a new, noncommercial alternative to Goodreads that is only available as a mobile app. It's great for book lovers but has little support for a localized presence, and it doesn't offer tools for integration with websites.
- *Hopefully your own website* allows customer book reviews and comments.

Business and Professional Networking Communities

Business and professional networking communities are places to share serious essays, professional news, and videos and presentations and to build a following based on your personal and organizational expertise. Platforms like this are for professional discourse, not informal conversations. If your service community includes businesses and professional groups, or you want to initiate relationships with these groups, professional networks are a terrific place to be.

Examples of business and professional networking communities: LinkedIn and Slideshare (now owned by LinkedIn, along with Lynda.com). Meetup.com gets an honorable mention because it is a useful way for entrepreneurs to find out about your programming.

Recommendation and Review Communities

They're not truly social media, but recommendation and review communities shouldn't be ignored because chances are high that customers and constituents are talking to you and about you. Typically you can't respond as your library until you have verified your official responsibility through a phone call to your publicly posted phone number or via a code sent via the mail to your location.

If you have to pick and choose, go with Google My Business, as the reviews and your responses (or silence) are visible every time the public searches for your library. If you have multiple libraries in your system, I recommend setting up accounts and alerts for all your libraries, not just the primary one. Note that you cannot remove reviews; you can only respond.

Notable recommendation and review sites to monitor: Google My Business,[15] Yelp,[16] and Wikipedia.

I've included Wikipedia because many online maps and directories pull from it. It's good to claim these pages too, not because of reviews or conversations, but because the information may be outdated or incorrect. Library-specific sources may pull from your OCLC listing.

Teen Communities

In America, a whopping 92 percent of teens ages thirteen to seventeen report going online daily, 71 percent of teens on Facebook, 52 percent on Instagram, and 41 percent on Snapchat. Social media would seem to be the perfect place for a library to interact with area youth.[17] And yet many libraries find that connecting with this age group online is challenging.

There are a few firsthand accounts published by teens that suggest that most are only on social media to be with friends.[18] These three young people don't represent all teens, but if "friends-only" is indeed common, this would explain the difficulty many libraries have engaging with youth online, as well as make the spontaneity and authenticity of voice even more important.

Success is possible, especially if your goals are "being there" and are less focused on marketing the library. Early Snapchat adopter libraries report that regular posts about what goes on behind the scenes help teens and millennials feel more comfortable about visiting the library. Ten-second candid book review? Equipment unboxing? Try it and see what happens.

Arlington new media librarian Alex Zealand puts it this way: "You can best reach your teens on social media if you have already reached them in person. Then instead of making a huge effort to reach out to them through social media, you're simply allowing them access to you in a different way. You're just there, in that social media space, if they need you."[19]

Another approach is to recruit teen advocates and employees as team writers for the library teen accounts. The teens would get professional social media training and mentorship, and the library wins by having authentic, local voices contributing to the account. This is our approach here at Pima County Public Library, and the youth ownership makes up for their sometimes infrequent posts.

It's a moving target, but currently Snapchat, Instagram, and Tumblr have the heaviest use by teens, along with Twitter and instant messaging apps. The best way to find out what your area youth are using, however, is to simply ask them where they are active or offer a humorous way to vote in your teen spaces. One researcher asked teens to send screenshots of their mobile phone home screen and it was quite illuminating to see what apps teens have on that first screen.[20]

Social Media Similarities and Differences

Facebook

The Pew Research Center reports that Facebook is by far the most popular social media platform, with the broadest adoption among Americans of all ages and backgrounds.[21] It also offers the most comprehensive selection of tools. Facebook wants to be everything: the way you stay in touch with friends and family, your event calendar, your preferred source of news, your blog platform, your business customer service messaging, your instant messaging, your group and organizational forum, and your source of video learning and entertainment. For free.

However, for libraries there is a trade-off. On one hand, you have the largest, widest access and the most ways to communicate. On the other hand, the learning curve is higher, it is by far the most time-consuming, and all business/organization posts are subject to heavy filtering by Facebook's EDGE algorithm.[22] On average, according to *Adweek*, a typical post is seen by only 5 percent of a Facebook page's active "Likes."[23] This means that two thousand people may have Liked your page, but on average, only one hundred people will actually see a post.[24] If you consistently beat that 5 percent, you are doing well. These numbers will improve significantly if you can afford to pay for ads and boost posts.

Below is an example of a post that was a success for one of our library branches (see figure 1.1). It reached over 270 percent of the branch's following and was a big success for their page. What about it worked on Facebook that day?

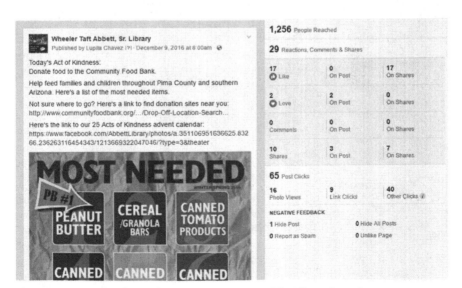

Figure 1.1.   **Facebook post from a Pima County Public Library branch**

How does Facebook decide whether to show your post to a reader? Facebook uses an algorithm, or computational formula, that takes into account:

- interest of reader in page (Has the reader interacted with you in the last month?)
- post virality (Do the first readers respond strongly to it? Or is there no reaction?)
- past success (Has your page been consistently interesting and engaging?)
- type (Videos and photos are more successful than text and links.)
- how new the post is (Is it more than an hour old?)

Notice that there is little in the algorithm about the actual content. It's mostly about how your readers respond to the post and have responded to your page in the last month. This makes it our job to consistently post timely information that our readers value and expect from their library.

The other point here is that important, meaty posts on topics like voter information will do better if you are also posting things of "human interest" like pop culture and library/reader/learning humor. Or in this case (above), information of civic interest not directly related to library services.

In other words, Facebook rewards pages that know what will interest their audience. It's up to us to find the sweet spots where our community's interests and the library's story intersect. Facebook success requires a commitment to listening to your readers, learning what works, and keeping up with Facebook's newsfeed tweaks. Facebook can be powerful, but it requires a real investment in staff time to reach its potential for your library.

Incompatibility: Facebook rewards those who post directly using its website or app and not with third-party scheduling managers such as Hootsuite, Buffer, or IFTTT. Thankfully we can now save drafts and schedule posts right from Facebook. One exception is Instagram, for which there is no penalty for cross-posting to Facebook, since Facebook owns it. For libraries on Facebook, this means that adding a new social media service is a big decision since they cannot all be easily managed from one place.

Future outlook: As soon as a new app becomes popular, Facebook either buys it (Instagram, WhatsApp) or develops its own version of the service. In 2016, they redesigned Notes and Events to better compete with blogs and Meetup[25] and created Facebook Live and Instagram Stories to compete with Snapchat. They are reportedly developing tools for job hunters and recruiters to compete with LinkedIn. I believe Facebook will continue to offer the most value to libraries, especially those who can assign staff who have time to stay on top of best practices and experiment with what works. If your library can purchase ads, Facebook will be even more rewarding. What other social media platforms are libraries using (see figure 1.2)?

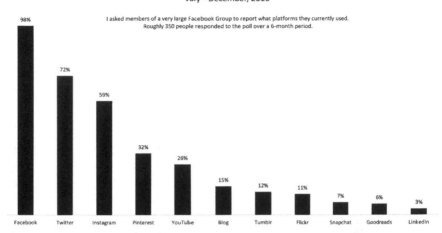

Figure 1.2. **Library social media usage**

Twitter

It is unsurprising that Twitter has been heavily adopted by American libraries, as some of its early champions were authors like Neil Gaiman and Margaret Atwood. Harry Potter author J. K. Rowling uses it as her primary way to communicate with fans. Fans in turn get glimpses into the world of the writer: their joys, anxieties, musings, and interests.[26] Twitter has also proved useful as a way to foster direct relationships with local reporters looking for their next feature.

Twitter has a bad rap for banality, but its readers value the platform for the closeness it affords to the famous and infamous, its immediacy for news, and snappy wordplay. Because of Twitter, I can read what influential librarians are reading the same day they do and perhaps have a conversation with them about it.

Flexibility: For libraries, another part of the appeal is that it takes far less time to write for Twitter than Facebook, and Twitter is more tolerant of traditional marketing, such as events announcements and links to blog posts. It is also easier to schedule and cross-post to services like LinkedIn and Google+ using tools like Hootsuite, Buffer, or IFTTT.

Demographics: Twitter can be a way to reach working-age people with above-average incomes and education.[27] The most current statistics may be found at www.pewinternet.org, under the "Science and Internet" tab. It varies by community, but you may also find local teens on Twitter as well.

Outlook: Today, much of the early uniqueness is gone and worries about privacy and bullying[28] have cut into its readership. The 2016 presidential election brought

Twitter back into the limelight as candidates sometimes used it to circumvent contact with traditional news media and speak directly to their followers; however, financial analysts have worries about Twitter's future.[29]

Bottom line? If your local community is active on Twitter, its still-large readership, its role in breaking news, and its flexibility make it a good second choice after Facebook.

Pinterest

Pinterest is a way anyone can create their own virtual inspiration boards, museums, shopping lists, and visual bookmarks. Everyone is a curator. If you have strong visual collections to showcase, collect craft activity ideas, or post book reviews, Pinterest can be rewarding.

On the other hand, your geographic location and the date of a post are not valued at all here, so it is much less useful for hyper-local or time-sensitive posts. Hashtags are not useful, and actual conversations are rare. People pin and repin images but rarely write to one another. Pinterest has excellent tools for pinning from websites but does not encourage cross-posting to other platforms.

Demographics: Pinterest's heaviest use comes from well-educated women under the age of fifty,[30] and its use is holding steady, possibly because it has no direct competitors. The most current statistics may be found at www.pewinternet.org, under the "Science and Internet" tab.

Some library uses include:

- collecting story-time and craft ideas where parents and teachers can access them
- boards with ideas and support for other programming, like STEM and arts classes
- pinning book covers for readers' advisory and discussion groups
- support for area fandoms
- images from special collections and archives
- showcasing library buildings and public art now and in history
- reading and library humor
- information on local authors and illustrators
- collaborations with the public, such as sharing book spine poetry

Instagram

Unlike Flickr or Pinterest, Instagram does not allow for collections of images organized by "boards" or albums, but this is also its strength. People who are overwhelmed by Facebook love the simplicity of Instagram. There is far less noise, fewer ads, and more original content. Whereas on Facebook a friend might post all sixty photos of their trip to Scotland, the same friend will save their favorites for Instagram. A smartphone or tablet is required for posting; you cannot use a Mac or PC.

Use Instagram to establish a reality-based visual identity for your library and tell a deeper story of what you contribute to your service area.

You can use Instagram to send visual messages like: "We are a welcoming space (staff, customers, events)," "We love where we live and make things better (photos with a sense of place, sense of purpose)," "We know books and reading (story time, book recommendations, and reader in-jokes)," and "We will surprise you (new initiatives, unusual events, anything timely)."

Demographics: Some of the audiences you may find here are women, teens and people under the age of twenty-nine, and African American and Hispanic people.[31] Instagram has recently seen an increase in growth of rural users. The most current statistics may be found at www.pewinternet.org, under the "Science and Internet" tab.

Common library uses include series, such as weekly posts of staff shown with books they review; you-are-there photographs of events; pop culture quotes; visual book and reading humor such as #bookfacefriday and "shelfies" (selfies in front of personal or special bookshelves); behind-the-scenes work; short videos; images from archives and special collections; and many of the uses listed (above) for Pinterest. Showcase your buildings, neighborhood, city, staff, customers, and history, and you will do well.

Tumblr

Like the geekier Reddit, Tumblr is a platform where people who love the same things can share and reshare easily. Niche communities like book, movie, game, music, comic, and TV show fandoms gather here to share (and reshare) the GIFs and memes they have created. Young adult novel fans will find that many of their favorite authors are very active on Tumblr,[32] as are art, design, illustration, and historical artifact blogs.

The libraries and librarians posting to Tumblr are so well networked they call themselves "Tumblarians."[33] What kinds of libraries are there? In a 2015 survey, Katie Elson Anderson determined that 45 percent of the libraries were public, 21 percent were special collections libraries, and 11 percent were academic libraries.[34]

Tumblr does not require real names and allows multiple accounts, which frees members up to experiment with interests and personas the same way gaming does. The anonymity also makes it a place where teens and young adults feel safe sharing vulnerabilities, usually in a humorous way.

Demographics: The largest users of Tumblr are non-white urban youth and young adults[35] and members of pop culture book, movie, and gaming fandoms.

Use Tumblr to reach a younger audience and wow them with the visual delights and hidden treasures of your collection. Like Instagram, you can also use Tumblr to send visual messages like: "We are a welcoming space," "We love where we live and make things better," "Our collection is fascinating," "We know books and reading," and "We will surprise you." Additionally, Tumblr has a unique capability of interest to libraries: you can allow readers to ask questions privately, then answer them publicly as a blog post.

Snapchat

Snapchat is growing the fastest among teens and young adults,[36] so some libraries that serve youth are learning its ins and outs. The activity is spontaneous in the extreme, consisting of short, live photos or video that only stay accessible for twenty-four hours.

Teens appreciate the quick, intimate sharing of real-life moments with friends, uninterrupted by advertisements or other unrelated information. The platform offers relative privacy (there's no search) and lacks the kinds of social labeling typical of Facebook (number of friends, relationship, location, etc.).[37]

The libraries on Snapchat are doing what the teens do: sharing snippets of fun and interesting happenings at the library.

Even if your library doesn't become active on Snapchat, it is possible to create "geo-filters," overlays that become possible when a Snapchatter visits your library.[38] When they open the app to post what they're doing to their friends, they can select an overlay that you or your community has designed. Overlays with logos or other branding are costly, so keep it informal.

Playbuzz

Is this a platform? Yes, but not a social one. It bills itself as "an authoring & distribution platform for interactive storytelling," which is to say a place with tools and templates for making interactive, playful web content and sharing or embedding it on other webpages or social media. The difference between it and other publishing platforms with widget makers is that it is not social on its own—you have to embed what you make somewhere else.

SO WHICH SOCIAL MEDIA
PLATFORM(S) SHOULD WE CHOOSE?

Remember the audience/message worksheet in the beginning of this chapter? Think back to who you identified as your primary audiences and consider what platform(s) fit your needs, and what the different services offer.

There are other considerations. Where is your staff strong? Is your staff unusually skilled in photography or visual arts? Video making? Readers' advisory? Music? Choose a platform that will showcase where your library staff already excel.

There may also be regional differences that determine what kinds of platform(s) fit your needs. What are your programming partners using? Make a list of your programming partners and other simpatico organizations or businesses, then visit their websites to see what platforms they are active on. Make a tally to see where local energy already exists.

FINAL THOUGHTS AND RECOMMENDATIONS

Even if the top five social media companies fail tomorrow your efforts will not be in vain because you will have learned how to be the library online in all its richness, something that will remain important as long as there is an Internet.

Regardless of what platform you choose, the recipe for success is the same:

1. Know your audience and what you have to say.
2. Remain in touch with your audience's changing needs and interests.
3. Be there: post frequently, respond quickly, be spontaneous, be local.
4. Be real: authentic, interesting, and helpful.
5. Be the show and not the commercial.[39]
6. Keep experimenting with content; keep it fresh.
7. Have fun and show your passion: tell stories with heart and emotion.

Another way to choose a social media platform is to create a matrix that charts key points for easy comparison. Here, for example, are the top three platforms with comparison points listed (see table 1.2).

Table 1.2. Platform Evaluation Matrix

	Facebook	Twitter	Instagram
Market share of social media visits	72 percent of adult Internet users.	23 percent of adult Internet users.	28 percent of adult Internet users.
Number of active users	1.59 billion.	320 million.	400 million.
Who uses it: demographics	Facebook has the largest, broadest market share of all social media.	Twitter can be a way to reach working-age people with above-average incomes and education.	As of November 2016, the primary audience is young women, and Instagram is one of the few places to reach teens with any consistency. All income levels use Instagram.
Costs	Your time photographing, making videos, posting, and monitoring. It's the most time-consuming to use of all the platforms.	Your time photographing, making videos, posting, and monitoring.	Your time photographing, making videos, posting, and monitoring.
Levels of access	Five levels of account access.	EVERYONE has the same level of access.	EVERYONE has the same level of access.
Security	Have a strong password and opt in to login approval (smartphone required).	Have a strong password and opt in to login verification if you have a smartphone.	Have a strong password.
Special equipment needed	Digital camera or camera-phone highly recommended.	Digital camera or camera-phone highly recommended.	Smartphone or tablet. You can't use a desktop or laptop for posting to Instagram.
Useful third-party tools	Canva, the official Pages Manager smartphone app.	Canva, Hootsuite, Tagboard, Storify.	Geopiq ($) helps you find local influencers. Tailwind, for scheduling, monitoring, and analysis.

Why fans like it

Facebook wants to be everything: the way you stay in touch with friends and family, your event calendar, your preferred source of news, your blog platform, business customer service messaging, instant messaging, your group and organizational forum, and your source of video learning and entertainment.

Twitter is still the platform of choice for news media and authors and rewards those who post with creativity, wit, and real voice.

Twitter's strength is its immediacy and access to news as it happens. Following is not reciprocal so it is possible to follow celebrities and influential people in your fields of interest.

Twitter used to be text-only short messages but, with its purchase of Periscope, has made a big investment in streaming video too.

News and posts in real time can be visceral, and it is probably the closest many of us will get to authors, celebrities, and other influential people.

The least "noisy" interface, it feels clean and simple, especially compared with Facebook.

Instagram fans love to scroll through captivating, original photographs and short videos, usually ones taken recently. They can "like" or comment on the images but not share them easily, so there is very little recycled content.

(Continued)

Table 1.2. *(Continued)*

	Facebook	Twitter	Instagram
Strategic opportunities for the library	Raise awareness of today's libraries, customer service, send people to library website, readers' advisory, connect people to the best online resources, build pride in community, support other civic organizations, have book/learning-centric fun. Events system is very good for your biggest events. Once you build an audience you can invite public participation with posts like "What two words would you like to tell your sixteen-year-old self?" and simple poetry projects like haiku and bookshelf poetry.	Sharing breaking news and new website posts with working-age adults, raise awareness of today's libraries, customer service, send people to library website, readers' advisory, connect people to the best online resources, build price in community, support other civic organizations, have book/learning-centric fun. Consider live reporting from your great events.	Reach a younger audience the way they like to communicate: visually. Position your library as fun, nerdy, welcoming, and surprising. Once you build an audience, you can invite public participation with posts asking for photo contributions via hashtag, like "What does your TBR stack look like?" or "Show us where you keep your library card."
What's good to post?	Images, videos, quotes, events, bookish/tech news, humor, blog posts, helpful "did you know" links, challenges.	Real-time and just-in-time news, book cleverness, musings, website blog posts, cross-posts from Instagram.	Reality-based visual identity for your library with your best, funniest, most beautiful photos or videos.

How your following builds; how do people find your account?			
Your posts (photos, videos, events, humor) get shared—GREAT content.	Your posts (photos, videos, quotes, wittiness) get shared—GREAT content.	Plan series posts that have a built-in hashtag audience, such as #bookfacefriday or #staffpicks hashtags.
Facebook uses keywords to suggest your page. Make sure your page's "about" information is fully fleshed out and that all photos have a caption—metadata and posting regularly.	Use hashtags that already have a following—discoverability.	Cross-post to a few other social media platforms, like Facebook or Twitter.
Your allies and programming partners tag you (or you tag them)—networking.	Your allies and programming partners tag you (or you tag them)—networking.	Instagram will suggest your account to people based on shared interest and keywords—account activity.
Word of mouth at public service desk and ads that promote the page, a post, event, etc.—personal contact.	Word of mouth at public service desks and ads that promote the page, a post, event, etc.—personal contact.	Your allies and programming partners tag you (or you tag them)—networking.

NOTES

1. "A Seed Library Comes to the Old Pueblo," Pima County Public Library, last modified May 14, 2015, accessed December 5, 2016, www.library.pima.gov/blogs/post/a-seed-library -comes-to-the-old-pueblo/.

2. "Seed Library," Pima County Public Library, accessed December 5, 2016, www.library .pima.gov/browse_program/seed-library/; "Seed Library of Pima County Public Library," accessed December 5, 2016, www.facebook.com/PimaSeedLibrary/.

3. Readers may wonder why we did not simply give the Seed Library Team access to the system-wide Facebook page instead of starting a fresh one for them. At the time we were discussing whether subject-specific pages (teen services, Spanish services) would be more effective than branch pages, where the growth was limited by the geographic service area. Luckily we have the authority to add new accounts and were able to experiment with a separate seed library page.

4. Seed Library Facebook Team: Justine Hernandez, Tenecia Phillips, Kelly Wilson, Rachel Winch, Elizabeth Langley, and Susannah Connor.

5. We opened our first accounts in 2006, and I took them over in 2009.

6. "International Seed Library Forum Schedule of Events," Pima County Public Library, last modified March 31, 2015, accessed December 5, 2016, www.library.pima.gov/blogs/post/ islf2015-schedule/; "Tucson Hosts International Seed Library Forum May 3–6," Pima County Public Library, last modified March 31, 2013, accessed December 5, 2016, www.library.pima. gov/news/tucson-hosting-first-international-seed-library-forum-in-may/.

7. "Tucson, UNESCO City of Gastronomy," City of Tucson, last modified November 17, 2016, accessed December 5, 2016, www.tucsonaz.gov/integrated-planning/tucson-unesco-city-gastronomy.

8. Sarah Durham, *Brandraising* (San Francisco: Jossey-Bass, 2010); David A. Aaker, *Leadership* (New York: The Free Press, 2000); Elisabeth Doucett, *Creating Your Library Brand* (Chicago: American Library Association, 2008).

9. Ask me what happened when a staff member mistakenly flew the flag upside down on the day of the 2016 Electoral College vote.

10. Ryan Dube, "Here Are the Fastest Growing Social Networks You Need to Join," Make Use Of, September 4, 2015, accessed December 6, 2016, www.makeuseof.com/tag/7-fastest -growing-social-networks-according-google-trends/.

11. For example, here are some Snapchat statistics: Christina Newberry, "Top Snapchat Demographics That Matter to Social Media Marketers," Hootsuite Blog, last modified August 24, 2016, accessed December 7, 2016, blog.hootsuite.com/snapchat-demographics/.

12. "Teens Have a Smart Reason for Abandoning Facebook and Twitter," Quartz, last modified February 13, 2016, accessed December 30, 2016, qz.com/613640/teens-have-a -smart-reason-for-abandoning-facebook-and-twitter/.

13. "Organizations > Libraries Groups," Goodreads, 2016, accessed December 6, 2016, www.goodreads.com/group/subtopic/100-libraries; Molly McCardle, "Will Librarians Still Use Goodreads?" *Library Journal*, April 2, 2013, accessed December 6, 2016, reviews.li braryjournal.com/2013/04/in-the-bookroom/post/will-librarians-still-use-goodreads/; Nate Hoffelder, "Move over BookBub, Fussy Librarian—Goodreads Is Getting into EBook Discounts," *The Digital Reader*, May 17, 2016, accessed December 6, 2016, the-digital-reader .com/2016/05/17/move-over-bookbub-fussy-librarian-goodreads-is-getting-into-ebook-dis counts/; Lexi Pandell, "In Sunday Sketching, Christoph Niemann Tells the Brutal Truth

about the Creative Process," *Wired*, May 19, 2016, accessed December 6, 2016, www.wired .com/2016/05/goodreads-selling-books/.

14. "How Do I Add a Goodreads Tab to My Facebook Page?" Goodreads, 2016, accessed December 6, 2016, www.goodreads.com/help/show/108-how-do-i-add-a-goodreads-tab-to my-facebook-page.

15. "Google Business Page Management & Insights—Google My Business," Google, accessed December 6, 2016, www.google.com/business/how-it-works/.

16. "Claiming Your Business," Yelp, 2004, accessed December 6, 2016, biz.yelp.com/sup port/claiming.

17. Amanda Lenhart, "Teens, Social Media & Technology Overview 2015," Pew Research Center, Internet & Science, Tech, April 9, 2015, accessed December 29, 2016, www.pew internet.org/2015/04/09/teens-social-media-technology-2015/.

18. Andrew Watts, "A Teenager's View on Social Media," Backchannel, January 3, 2015, accessed December 6, 2016, backchannel.com/a-teenagers-view-on-social-media -1df945c09ac6#.uxjewoxlo; Sophie Laing, "This Gen-Z Teenager Explains Why and How She Uses Various Social Media Platforms," Social Media Week, June 24, 2015, accessed December 29, 2016, socialmediaweek.org/blog/2015/06/gen-z-social-platforms/; "Teens Have a Smart Reason," Quartz.

19. "Libraries & Social Media Facebook Group," Facebook, April 13, 2016, accessed December 30, 2016, www.facebook.com/groups/LibrarySocial/permalink/480215582169400/? match=dGVlbnMsdGVlbbg%3D%3D.

20. "Teens Have a Smart Reason," Quartz.

21. Seventy-nine percent of online adults in America use Facebook. The nearest popular platform is Instagram, at 32 percent. Source: "Social Media Update 2016," Pew Research Center, Internet & Science, Tech, November 11, 2016, accessed December 6, 2016, www .pewinternet.org/2016/11/11/social-media-update-2016/.

22. Andrew Hutchinson, "How Facebook's News Feed Works—as Explained by Facebook," Social Media Today, May 30, 2016, accessed December 6, 2016, www.socialmediatoday.com/ social-networks/how-facebooks-news-feed-works-explained-facebook; "Facebook Newsfeed Algorithm Change History—2016 Update," Wallaroo Media, November 15, 2016, accessed December 6, 2016, wallaroomedia.com/facebook-newsfeed-algorithm-change-history/.

23. David Cohen, "Organic Growth Becomes More Elusive on Facebook (study)," *Adweek*, January 5, 2016, accessed December 6, 2016, www.adweek.com/socialtimes/locowise-decem ber-2015/632367; David Cohen, "Media Companies' Reach per Facebook Post Plummeting in 2016 (study)," *Adweek*, June 8, 2016, accessed December 6, 2016, www.adweek.com/ socialtimes/socialflow-media-reach-facebook-study/640587.

24. I'm oversimplifying this a bit. The formula is actually the number of people who have liked, commented, or shared your post divided by the number of people who saw it. The formula is explained very well here: "How to Calculate Reach of Your Facebook Posts to Your Fans," Digitalks, July 27, 2013, accessed December 6, 2016, www.digitalks.me/tools/ facebook-insights/how-to-calculate-reach-of-your-facebook-posts-to-your-fans/.

25. Lisa Waite Bunker, "12 Tips to Make Facebook Events Successful for Your Library," 5-Minute Librarian, December 12, 2016, accessed December 27, 2016, www.5minlib .com/2016/12/12-tips-to-make-facebook-events.html.

26. Mensah Demary describes it well: "In Search of Lost Tweets: On Being a Writer on Twitter," Electric Literature, April 30, 2015, accessed December 6, 2016, electricliterature. com/in-search-of-lost-tweets-on-being-a-writer-on-twitter-8876864c6640#.312qlpia1.

27. "Social Media Update 2016," Pew Research Center.
28. Jessica Coccimiglio, "Tweeting While Female: Harassment, and How Twitter Can Fix It," Make Use Of, March 30, 2015, accessed December 6, 2016, www.makeuseof.com/tag/abuse-twitter-happens-twitter-can-fix/.
29. Deborah Findling, Lionel Bonaventure, and Fred Imbert, "Analysts to Twitter: 'Hope Is Not a Strategy,'" Market Insider (CNBC), May 24, 2016, www.cnbc.com/2016/05/24/analysts-to-twitter-hope-is-not-a-strategy.html.
30. "Social Media Update 2016," Pew Research Center.
31. "Social Media Update 2016," Pew Research Center.
32. Carolyn Kellogg, "Tumblr: A Place for Readers and Favorite Authors to Connect," *Los Angeles Times*, April 15, 2015, accessed December 30, 2016, www.latimes.com/books/jacketcopy/la-et-jc-festival-tumblr-lit-20150415-story.html.
33. "Tumblarians on Tumblr," Tumblr, 2016, accessed December 30, 2016, www.tumblr.com/tagged/tumblarians.
34. Katie Elson Anderson, "Libraries and Tumblr: A Quantitative Analysis," *Reference Services Review*, 2015.
35. "Mobile Messaging and Social Media 2015: Main Findings," Pew Research Center: Internet, Science and Tech, August 19, 2015, accessed December 7, 2016, www.pewinternet.org/2015/08/19/mobile-messaging-and-social-media-2015-main-findings/.
36. "Topic: Snapchat," Statista, November 17, 2016, accessed December 6, 2016, www.statista.com/topics/2882/snapchat.
37. Watts, "A Teenager's View."
38. "Snapchat Geofilters for Your Public Library," NJSL Direct, September 7, 2016, accessed December 7, 2016, njsldirect.org/looking-good-snapchat-geofilters-public-library/.
39. "Want to Win with Content Marketing? Stick to These 3 Basics," Hootsuite Blogs, July 21, 2014, accessed December 6, 2016, blog.hootsuite.com/want-to-win-at-content-marketing-stick-to-these-3-basics/.

BIBLIOGRAPHY

Aaker, David A. *Leadership*. New York: The Free Press, 2000.
Anderson, Katie Elson. "Libraries and Tumblr: A Quantitative Analysis." *Reference Services Review*. 2015.
Bunker, Lisa Waite. "12 Tips to Make Facebook Events Successful for Your Library." 5-Minute Librarian. December 12, 2016, accessed December 27, 2016. www.5minlib.com/2016/12/12-tips-to-make-facebook-events.html.
City of Tucson. "Tucson, UNESCO City of Gastronomy." Last modified November 17, 2016, accessed December 5, 2016. www.tucsonaz.gov/integrated-planning/tucson-unesco-city-gastronomy.
"Claiming Your Business." Yelp. 2004, accessed December 6, 2016. biz.yelp.com/support/claiming.
Coccimiglio, Jessica. "Tweeting While Female: Harassment, and How Twitter Can Fix It." Make Use Of. March 30, 2015, accessed December 6, 2016. www.makeuseof.com/tag/abuse-twitter-happens-twitter-can-fix/.
Cohen, David. "Media Companies' Reach per Facebook Post Plummeting in 2016 (study)." *Adweek*. June 8, 2016, accessed December 6, 2016. www.adweek.com/socialtimes/socialflow-media-reach-facebook-study/640587.

———. "Organic Growth Becomes More Elusive on Facebook (study)." *Adweek*, January 5, 2016, accessed December 6, 2016. www.adweek.com/socialtimes/locowise-decem ber-2015/632367.

Doucett, Elisabeth. *Creating Your Library Brand*. Chicago: American Library Association, 2008.

Dube, Ryan. "Here Are the Fastest Growing Social Networks You Need to Join." Make Use Of. September 4, 2015, accessed December 6, 2016. www.makeuseof.com/tag/7-fastest -growing-social-networks-according-google-trends/.

Durham, Sarah. *Brandraising*. San Francisco: Jossey-Bass, 2010.

"Facebook Newsfeed Algorithm Change History—2016 Update." Wallaroo Media. November 15, 2016, accessed December 6, 2016. wallaroomedia.com/facebook-newsfeed -algorithm-change-history/.

Findling, Deborah, Lionel Bonaventure, and Fred Imbert. "Analysts to Twitter: 'Hope Is Not a Strategy.'" Market Insider (CNBC), May 24, 2016. www.cnbc.com/2016/05/24/analysts -to-twitter-hope-is-not-a-strategy.html.

"Google Business Page Management & Insights—Google My Business." Google, accessed December 6, 2016. www.google.com/business/how-it-works/.

Hoffelder, Nate. "Move over BookBub, Fussy Librarian—Goodreads Is Getting into EBook Discounts." *The Digital Reader*. May 17, 2016, accessed December 6, 2016. the-digital -reader.com/2016/05/17/move-over-bookbub-fussy-librarian-goodreads-is-getting-into -ebook-discounts/.

"How Do I Add a Goodreads Tab to My Facebook Page?" Goodreads. 2016, accessed December 6, 2016. www.goodreads.com/help/show/108-how-do-i-add-a-goodreads-tab-to -my-facebook-page.

"How to Calculate Reach of Your Facebook Posts to Your Fans." Digitalks. July 27, 2013, accessed December 6, 2016. www.digitalks.me/tools/facebook-insights/how-to-calculate -reach-of-your-facebook-posts-to-your-fans/.

Hutchinson, Andrew. "How Facebook's News Feed Works—as Explained by Facebook." Social Media Today. May 30, 2016, accessed December 6, 2016. www.socialmediatoday.com/ social-networks/how-facebooks-news-feed-works-explained-facebook.

"In Search of Lost Tweets: On Being a Writer on Twitter." Electric Literature. April 30, 2015, accessed December 6, 2016. electricliterature.com/in-search-of-lost-tweets-on-being-a -writer-on-twitter-8876864c6640#.312qlpia1.

Kellogg, Carolyn. "Tumblr: A Place for Readers and Favorite Authors to Connect." *Los Angeles Times*. April 15, 2015, accessed December 30, 2016. www.latimes.com/books/jacketcopy/ la-et-jc-festival-tumblr-lit-20150415-story.html.

Laing, Sophie. "This Gen-Z Teenager Explains Why and How She Uses Various Social Media Platforms." Social Media Week. June 24, 2015, accessed December 29, 2016. socialmedia week.org/blog/2015/06/gen-z-social-platforms/.

Lenhart, Amanda. "Teens, Social Media & Technology Overview 2015." Pew Research Center, Internet & Science, Tech. April 9, 2015, accessed December 29, 2016. www.pewinter net.org/2015/04/09/teens-social-media-technology-2015/.

"Libraries & Social Media Facebook Group." Facebook. April 13, 2016, accessed December 30, 2016. www.facebook.com/groups/LibrarySocial/permalink/480215582169400/?match =dGVlbnMdGVlbg%3D%3D.

McCardle, Molly. "Will Librarians Still Use Goodreads?" *Library Journal*. April 2, 2013, accessed December 6, 2016, reviews.libraryjournal.com/2013/04/in-the-bookroom/post/ will-librarians-still-use-goodreads/.

"Mobile Messaging and Social Media 2015: Main Findings." Pew Research Center: Internet, Science and Tech. August 19, 2015, accessed December 7, 2016. www.pewinternet .org/2015/08/19/mobile-messaging-and-social-media-2015-main-findings/.

Newberry, Christina. "Top Snapchat Demographics That Matter to Social Media Marketers." Hootsuite Blog. Last modified August 24, 2016, accessed December 7, 2016. blog.hootsuite.com/snapchat-demographics.

"Organizations > Libraries Groups." Goodreads. 2016, accessed December 6, 2016. www .goodreads.com/group/subtopic/100-libraries.

Pandell, Lexi. "In Sunday Sketching, Christoph Niemann Tells the Brutal Truth about the Creative Process." *Wired*. May 19, 2016, accessed December 6, 2016. www.wired .com/2016/05/goodreads-selling-books/.

Pima County Public Library. "International Seed Library Forum Schedule of Events." Last modified March 31, 2015, accessed December 5, 2016. www.library.pima.gov/blogs/post/ islf2015-schedule/.

———. "Seed Library." Accessed December 5, 2016. www.library.pima.gov/browse_program/ seed-library/.

———.A Seed Library Comes to the Old Pueblo." Last modified May 14, 2015, accessed December 5, 2016. www.library.pima.gov/blogs/post/a-seed-library-comes-to-the-old -pueblo/.

———. "Seed Library of Pima County Public Library." Accessed December 5, 2016. www .facebook.com/PimaSeedLibrary/.

———. "Tucson Hosts International Seed Library Forum May 3–6." Last modified March 31, 2013, accessed December 5, 2016. www.library.pima.gov/news/tucson-hosting-first -international-seed-library-forum-in-may.

Quartz. "Teens Have a Smart Reason for Abandoning Facebook and Twitter." Last modified February 13, 2016, accessed December 30, 2016. qz.com/613640/teens-have-a-smart -reason-for-abandoning-facebook-and-twitter/.

"Snapchat Geofilters for Your Public Library." NJSL Direct. September 7, 2016, accessed December 7, 2016. njsldirect.org/looking-good-snapchat-geofilters-public-library/.

"Social Media Update 2016." Pew Research Center, Internet & Science, Tech. November 11, 2016, accessed December 6, 2016. www.pewinternet.org/2016/11/11/social-media -update-2016/.

"Topic: Snapchat." Statista. November 17, 2016, accessed December 6, 2016. www.statista .com/topics/2882/snapchat.

"Tumblarians on Tumblr." Tumblr. 2016, accessed December 30, 2016. www.tumblr.com/ tagged/tumblarians.

"Want to Win with Content Marketing? Stick to These 3 Basics." Hootsuite Blogs. July 21, 2014, accessed December 6, 2016. blog.hootsuite.com/want-to-win-at-content-marketing-stick-to-these-3-basics/.

Watts, Andrew. "A Teenager's View on Social Media." Backchannel. January 3, 2015, accessed December 6, 2016. backchannel.com/a-teenagers-view-on-social-media-1df945c09ac6# .uxjewoxlo.

2

From Broadcast to Conversation in an Academic Library

Laura Little, Andrew Lopez,
Jessica McCullough, and Rebecca Parmer

OVERVIEW

Our chapter focuses on how we use social media at Connecticut College as a tool to facilitate communication within our division (Information Services), with our campus, and with other communities. We describe the outlets and platforms we use and how we use them, the challenges we face, and future plans for building a broader community. Importantly, we also reflect on the role social media has played in strengthening our own working relationships, bringing together isolated units within our organization, as well as how work on this chapter itself provided an impulse to articulate goals and examine practices.

Connecticut College is a private, residential liberal arts college located in New London, Connecticut, halfway between New York City and Boston. The college offers fifty-six majors, minors, and certificates to nineteen hundred students. Library and technology services are merged into one division, Information Services (IS). While we work in a merged environment, silos exist between departments in the division due to physical separation, reporting structures, and different workplace cultures.

The chapter is organized chronologically, beginning with our nascent efforts in using social media for outreach. As we learned more about the social media landscape and our activities expanded, we faced challenges related to our internal divisional structure, the bureaucratization of our efforts, lack of recognition for this work, and questions surrounding the audiences we sought to engage. The chapter then details four areas that serve as case studies illustrating successes and failures: reaching the campus community through Facebook, students as content creators, engaging faculty, and interinstitutional community. We conclude with recommendations to other institutions that are looking to expand their social media activities.

EARLY DAYS: GETTING TOGETHER, BREACHING SILOS

The authors of this chapter are relatively new to the college; we started within a year of each other in 2012–2013 and represent three departments in IS: Instructional Technology, Research Support and Instruction, and Special Collections and Archives. Each of us were active social media users, having used social media personally and professionally at our previous jobs. Energized by our transitions to a new institutional context, we brought to our positions a desire to use social media as an extension of our work and an opportunity to build community. We saw social media as a dynamic form of outreach, with the potential to facilitate engagement and foster social innovation. We had the lofty notion that we could both meet individuals "when and where they were" and engage the campus across interest and affinity groups.

Like the libraries mentioned in Nancy Dowd's *Library Journal* article, "Social Media: Libraries Are Posting, but Is Anyone Listening?" IS's initial social media efforts were inconsistent and disconnected.[1] Within the division, there were a handful of independently managed accounts, including five unrelated Facebook pages, one Twitter account, and one blog. These accounts were largely focused on unidirectional broadcasting of informational content and lacked engagement with one another and with the larger community. Technically speaking, we weren't even listening to ourselves, and the disjointedness and lack of communication across channels was isolating and frustrating. This state of affairs led us to propose to our divisional head a single account that would be representative of our various efforts in one platform and that would allow us to aggregate and disseminate information under the divisional IS label.

Twitter, which seemed to offer relative ease of reposting from multiple streams and which was the outlet for local information favored by the college's Office of Communications, seemed the best choice for this purpose. We composed a formal proposal that articulated the following goals:

1. All Facebook and blog posts will be broadcast through the unified Twitter account, creating a lively stream of information that will reflect the breadth and depth of IS daily activities.
2. Ensure that the Twitter feed is not "unidirectional," that is, that IS is following other institutions on and off campus and retweeting content of interest to our community, thereby creating a richer resource for followers.
3. Ensure that existing IS Facebook pages "Like" other divisional/departmental pages so that we may help each other attain greater visibility and reach.
4. Maintain an active Twitter presence throughout the year.

In our impulse to engage with the broader campus as a single entity, we hoped to add a layer of cohesion and centrality—via Twitter—to the individual voices already present. To effectively aggregate content from diverse departments, we needed to hold regular meetings, establish a collaborative online workspace in Google Drive, follow the work being done in different IS departments, and keep up with the various social media accounts associated with IS and the college. These activities helped build lateral relationships within IS. This new collaboration thus had the inadvertent but important effect of building a cross-departmental community.

GETTING ORGANIZED, GETTING PROFESSIONAL: CREATING A SOCIAL MEDIA GUIDE

Motivated to augment our efforts and loath to reinvent the wheel, in January 2014, several members of the social media group attended the Library and Information Technology Association (LITA) Workshop on Strategic Social Media at American Library Association's 2014 midwinter conference.[2] At the workshop, Scott Young, Doralyn Rossmann, Angela Tate, and Mary Anne Hansen of Montana State University (MSU) Library presented on using social media strategically to build community online. The all-day workshop was so impressive we wrote about it in "Starting a New Twitter Account @ConnCollegeIS: With a Report from #ALAMW14," published in *Journal of Electronic Resources Librarianship*.[3]

One important takeaway from the LITA workshop was that we needed a social media guide to:

- articulate our goals for each platform,
- define ourselves as well as our audience, and
- provide examples of posting types and scheduling.

Using MSU's guide as a model,[4] we set about creating an IS-focused Social Media Guide, soliciting and compiling input from the gatekeepers of the various channels. In addition to the inventory of our many channels' names and web addresses, the guide lists who is responsible for posting, provides suggestions and examples of posts, delineates useful—local and global—hashtags, and includes a calendar of commemorative months and days we may wish to observe (created by a student worker).

The Social Media Guide is a living document that evolves according to our efforts and the changing nature of the social media landscape. It provides guidance about what we should be posting and when and attempts to sketch out a practical plan for connecting with students and others on and off campus. Creating it did take more time than anticipated, as we built buy-in from the various groups and individuals involved, but once established, and once the habit of consulting it took root, it became a useful source of guidance and a reminder of our goals.

GROWING PAINS

Our enthusiasm, unfortunately, was not all that would be required to sustain or expand efforts over the long term. Our well-meaning attempt to organize, codify,

and sustain our small group, including to add less-motivated staff from other departments, slowed our momentum and ultimately led to bureaucratization. Despite
having official policies and a formally recognized committee, time spent on social
media activities was not part of any member's job description and was unevenly acknowledged by department heads. Questions surrounding our audience and desire
to move beyond one-way communication also required us to step back and think
carefully about why and how we engaged in social media activities. This section
describes these challenges in more detail.

Internal Structures

Although initial efforts were the product of our ad hoc committee of social media
enthusiasts, under the directive of the vice president of IS, our role was formalized
in a policy statement in 2015.[5] The policy established a Social Media Committee
with representatives from each of the five teams within IS—Enterprise Systems,
Instructional Technology, IT Service Desk, Research Support and Instruction, Special Collections and Archives—and included the four authors of this chapter. The
intended purpose of a formal policy and committee was to provide guidelines for the
administration of official ISs social media channels. The policy also detailed the process by which new accounts and outlets could be created, requiring formal proposals
and approval by the vice president for IS and the Leadership Team (made up of
department heads). The formalization of our efforts from the highest position in our
division was important in validating our work, but it uncovered a tension between
the bureaucratization of social media use and the flexibility required to be successful.

Interest in the newly appointed committee varied. While some new members were
enthusiastic about discussing and generating content together, others were not. Lack
of interest can partly be attributed to the way in which some departments selected
members to join the committee: some were simply assigned to the committee regardless of experience or interest in social media. The group's size and composition de-
tracted from its effectiveness, and we struggled to generate interest and engagement
among committee members.

Policy and committee notwithstanding, social media activities were not, and
still are not, largely acknowledged by department heads. Our work in social media
is therefore not prioritized and is easily eclipsed by other duties. For example, in
midsemester when our social media presence should be at its strongest, we struggle
to post new content because our focus is directed to the more pressing tasks of teaching, student and faculty consultations, and working with researchers. While it is not
always easy to find time for social media activities, maintaining a fresh social media
guide can indicate the way forward and provide the structure needed to be proactive.

Audience

We struggled to define our audience. Were we targeting faculty? Students? Staff?
Through which channels? As we began actively expanding our social media program,

we realized that each platform seemed to have different audiences that interacted with content in specific ways. In order to better reach these followers, we needed to adapt our content on each platform accordingly. By creating diverse content specific to each social media platform, we find that we can reach a broader audience and increase the likelihood of engagement.

At the same time, fostering relationships is not only about creating content and clever posting but about engaging with others' content. On Twitter, for example, it's easy to interact with other organizations and public figures in an informative, conversational manner. We regularly tweet questions at other offices on campus, library vendors, and news organizations. When Jelani Cobb of the *New Yorker* came to campus for a much-anticipated discussion about free speech, we used Twitter to promote the event. By announcing the event, live tweeting the debate, and sharing the audio recording via Twitter afterward, we were able to interact with a dynamic cross section of our community, the Twitter community, and Jelani Cobb himself (see figure 2.1).[6]

On Instagram, on the other hand, we have a more intimate campus audience, dominated primarily by students, where we focus on people, spaces, and events on campus.

In order to better understand trends in our followers, we decided to maintain a record of the number of posts published weekly and the number of followers of each account. We monitor our production via a simple Google Sheet, shared among all members of the Social Media Committee and updated weekly by a student worker. While the document only provides quantitative snapshots of activity at specific points in time, we can use it to understand trends and impact. For example, we now know that followers increase at a higher rate in the first and last weeks of the academic year. And after a recent Instagram campaign for #NationalDictionaryDay, we learned that our followers increased by 8 percent, suggesting that this initiative was worth the time invested (see figure 2.2).

Expansion and Evolution

As our efforts came together in a centralized program, we began to think broadly about potential content, contributions, and contributors. We scheduled a regular monthly meeting with members of the IS Social Media Committee and then opened it up to any others interested in participating in social media activities as well. The Social Media Committee consists of six members, while our expanded monthly meeting includes up to fourteen staff and students. In expanding the group, we connected with staff and student workers across all departments within IS who were excited to participate. In particular, we hoped to create a space where contributors could come together for ideas and support, to discuss challenges and successes, to bolster and motivate one another, and to promote momentum and sustainability across our individual channels and collaborative efforts.

This expanded group has already shown promise. For example, when the issue of our limited success reaching students on Twitter was raised at one of these monthly

Figure 2.1.   Twitter interaction about campus event

meetings, a student staff member suggested that the group try Instagram, as students were more actively using it than they were Twitter. We turned our attention to this new channel (@shainlibrary) and found that the suggestion was a great one; the visually oriented platform allows us to showcase faces and places in the library and to interact more directly with students. By enthusiastically commenting on, "Liking," and reposting images from the community, we have been able not only to connect with a larger student community but also to generate more internal interest, excitement, and participation (see figure 2.3).

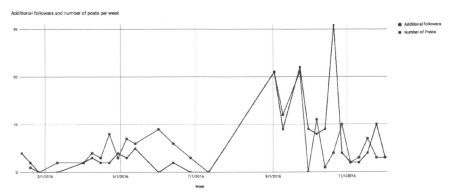

Figure 2.2.   **Graph showing the number of posts and number of additional followers by week**

Another result of our group discussions was the modification of our original Twitter account, rebranding it with a new name to better represent its content, focus, and contributing departments: @ConnCollLibTech. We also limited the automatic rebroadcast of content published on other channels, such as Instagram, Facebook, and Tumblr, after we discovered the differences in platform style and type sometimes resulted in the loss of meaning and context.

We often devote time in our monthly meetings to our Social Media Guide, comparing our recent work with the stated purpose and goals for the different plat-

Figure 2.3.   #HumansofShain Instagram post

forms, adding examples of successful posts or ideas for future reference, reviewing upcoming commemorative dates, and recording them in the document. Anyone interested in contributing to social media can view, add to, and edit it. As a result of this regular review, the guide has expanded significantly into a useful, regular reference resource.

SUCCESSES AND FAILURES

This section includes four "case studies" that discuss specific uses of different social media platforms in our organization, including Facebook, Twitter, Tumblr, and Word-Press blogs. We describe some of our successes (and a few failures), from the benefits and difficulties of involving students as content creators to the challenges of reaching multiple communities both within and outside of our campus. We hope these concrete examples provide insight into how we attempt to reach different communities through different platforms while also navigating the challenges outlined above.

Reaching the Campus Community on Facebook

A number of questions loomed as we considered how to use Facebook productively in our institutional context. When we joined Connecticut College, there were already five Facebook accounts in IS. We noticed that these officially related accounts hadn't even "Liked" each other as pages and were not in the habit of interacting much. A first order of business, therefore, was to get each of our own accounts to "Like" all of the other accounts and then to interact with one another. "Liking" or sharing posts within our own organization would hopefully convey our readiness to communicate with others.

Our inclination to post regularly and interact with others on campus and nearby, including other departments, schools, libraries, and local businesses, was initially restrained due to the lack of precedent in this area. Would it be okay for us to "Like" other organizations on behalf of our entire library? And what if we wanted to comment or ask questions? Each week we started seeking out several new area organizations on Facebook, "Liking" their pages, and interacting with some of their content in our "pages feed." Now it has become a component of our ongoing usage of Facebook. As an aside, one advantage of maintaining an up-to-date guide for social media usage is that it can make such practices explicit.

To give a sense of who makes up our community, consider some of these examples:

On campus:

- academic centers and departments
- athletic teams

- dining services
- student organizations
- support services

Nearby:

- community organizations
- cultural institutions
- local businesses
- local news media
- town, city, municipal services

Operating under the new idea in our library that part of building community through our Facebook page would involve moving beyond asymmetrical broadcast marketing toward listening to and interacting with others, we were eager to experiment with branching out. Listed above are examples of the kinds of Facebook pages in our community with which we began to interact.

To get a sense for how that plays out in terms of posting on the Charles E. Shain Library Facebook page, let's take a look at two examples. The first example is a picture of an igloo and a pyramid that students made in the snow on campus last winter (see figure 2.4). It has nothing to do with the library, but it was a cool thing a few students did that seemed worth recognizing. The second example is a picture of a senior honors student with lots of microfilm she was using for her research. It has everything to do with the library, and it represents a good opportunity to showcase library resources and services by posting about those who use them (see figure 2.5).

Each of these posts reached more than one thousand people and received more than thirty "Likes." In addition, they each attracted specific segments of our community and their friends and family to our page. This swell of interest had little to do with our organization specifically, except that we were now associated through Facebook with affiliated friends and loved ones. We became a vehicle for members of our community to see and interact with each other in a way that would not have been possible without us. Although it feels strange thinking about documenting things on our Facebook page that don't have any obvious connection to the library, we recognize that if we really want to play an active role in our community, we need to engage with the full range of our community's interests.

Takeaways:

- Seek out and "Like" campus and community organizations.
- Use the "pages feed" in Facebook to "Like" and interact with others' content.
- Post and interact regularly.
- Post about people's stories even if they don't concern the library directly.

Charles E. Shain Library
February 14, 2014 · ◉

The plot thickens...

#ShainLibrary

1,036 people reached   Boost Post

👍 Like   💬 Comment   ↗ Share   ◤ ▾

👍 Charles E. Shain Library, Cailyn Vogel, Ariana K. Taylor and 46 others

1 share

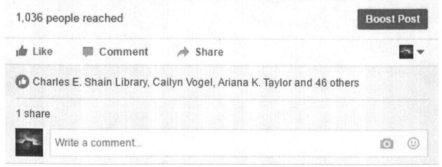

Write a comment...   📷   ☺

Figure 2.4.   Promoting student-built snow structures on Facebook

Charles E. Shain Library
Published by Andrew Lopez [?] · February 19 · 🌐

Big shout out to Senior Honors Researcher, Mia Haas-Goldberg!

Mia has made extensive use of inter-library loan & microfilm for her research on historic French newspaper representations of Algerians.

1,537 people reached   Boost Post

👍 Like   💬 Comment   ➤ Share

👍 Emily Aylward, Mitchell College Library and 30 others

Write a comment...   📷 😊

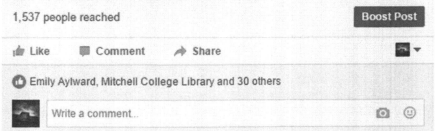

Figure 2.5.   Promoting student research on Facebook

Students as Content Creators

Connecticut College's language resource center, locally known as the Language and Culture Center, has a student staff of approximately fifteen students any given semester. Since they were already using social media at work (as could regularly be observed), leveraging students as content creators seemed an obvious way not only to delegate the work and make better use of the institution's investment in their wages, but also to diversify the perspectives represented on our channels (Facebook, Twitter, and later Instagram), to provide pre-professional opportunities to the staff, and—most importantly—to cultivate student ownership and belonging and thereby build a sense of community.

Initially, one student staff member was designated the gatekeeper for each of the center's two platforms, responsible for soliciting content from coworkers and posting it at regular intervals. While this approach ensured a steady stream of content, it created a workload imbalance, awkward hierarchical relations among equals, and a proliferation of e-mails encouraging, cajoling, and, in some cases, nagging staff members to provide their content. An idea proposed at a staff meeting resolved these issues: streamline and decentralize responsibility for posting. There would be no single gatekeeper; all student staff were provided with the necessary credentials to be editors of the center's channels. Students were asked to post one item each time they worked. Empowering the group in this way had multiple positive effects: greater quantity and variety of content, the elimination of lag time between ideas and posts, and equal participation by all.

As positive as this adjusted approach was, empowering students came with its own challenges, especially when we tried to replicate this model on other IS social media channels. When we tasked the Interlibrary Loan student workers with posting to the library's Instagram feed, we quickly realized that the work could not simply be outsourced; it needed to be supervised. Articulating expectations and reviewing the content that was generated required as much time as, if not more than, doing it oneself. However, given the equal time investment, the results were better—the student staff chose content of greater interest to their peers and were directly involved in crafting the center's profile (see figure 2.6).

Takeaways:

- Students bring a unique perspective to institutional social media.
- Expect to invest time providing guidance.
- Productivity and creativity can grow by giving students flexibility and autonomy.

Engaging Faculty

Engage is the blog for Instructional Technology at Connecticut College.[7] The blog's goals are to encourage faculty use of technology in teaching by highlighting

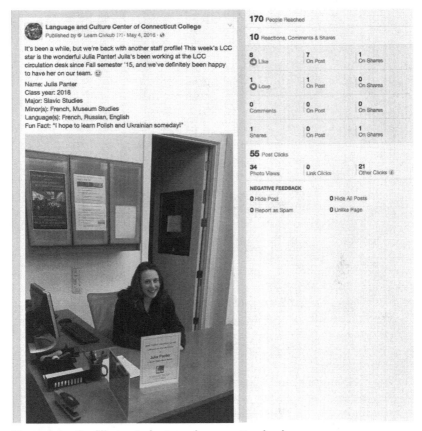

Figure 2.6.   Profiling a student employee on Facebook

interesting and creative uses of technology, share announcements of new services and products, and provide information about the Teaching with Technology workshop series. The *Engage* blog was created in July 2013 as a platform for sharing tools, pedagogical strategies, and stories of successful (or not successful) integration of technology in teaching. The scope also includes suggestions to improve productivity or save time—time that can then be used for more important activities such as teaching or research. As of this writing, the blog has gained more than 125 followers, many of whom are administrators, faculty, and staff at the college.

We found the best way for faculty to follow the blog is to hear about it from their faculty colleagues. While we worked hard to promote the blog through e-mail, regular workshops, mailings, and word of mouth, we had limited success. The most effective strategy for getting faculty to follow the blog was when faculty supporters recommended the blog on a faculty e-mail listserv. Any time a faculty member mentioned the blog at a meeting or in an e-mail to other faculty, the number of views spiked and we gained additional followers. Faculty were not only a passive audience for the blog's content but advocates for it and soon would become content creators as well.

Initially members of the Instructional Technology team created all the content for the blog, including occasional faculty contributions and a short-lived video interview series. We soon realized that for the blog to meet its goal of creating a platform to share success stories of pedagogical implementations of technology, we needed faculty to directly author content. At this time, faculty leaders of a new program, the Technology Fellows Program, were investigating platforms through which to share their experiences integrating technology into the classroom. We were able to connect our blogging platform and existing followers to this new program.

As part of the Technology Fellows Program now, each fellow is required to write blog posts. At the beginning of each semester, the four or five current fellows sign up to write two blog posts. We provide examples of "good" posts, explain the goal of the blog, and work with faculty to brainstorm topic ideas and edit their contributions. We have found that for some, publishing on a blog is a new and even overwhelming experience; the informal and conversational style in particular seems to be challenging for many. Through a collaboration between the faculty fellows and the Instructional Technology editors, we have found that faculty-authored blog posts are very popular and receive the most comments, mostly from faculty colleagues.

Takeaways:

- When the primary audience is faculty, faculty contribution and advocacy is an effective mechanism for gaining followers.
- Publishing on social media is still new to many people; sharing examples and offering support to contributors is important for publishing content appropriate for your audience and social media channel.

Interinstitutional Community: Libraries and Archives on Tumblr

The Linda Lear Center for Special Collections and Archives (LCSCA) has actively used social media as a tool for sharing collections, promoting events and activities, and engaging with patrons since 2010. Although Facebook was our initial platform of choice, we struggled to connect with an audience from the outset. Even with a fairly regular posting schedule and attempts at cross-promotion with other campus accounts, we had little sense of connection to our communities: few within or outside of the institution regularly interacted with our content by commenting or sharing posts, and communication with those that did felt formal and stilted. Lacking the community interaction we desired on Facebook's platform, we knew we needed to move on if we wanted to remain engaged and relevant.

In our search for a new platform, we considered several factors: audience, tone, and level of interaction. We wanted deeper engagement with collections, users, the campus community, and other institutions, but found the traditional blogging platforms formal and isolating; given our relative lack of success on Facebook, which at least came with a built-in audience base of campus departments using the same platform, would we be able to attract our audience to a new site? And even if we could get them to come, would we be able to achieve the level of interaction we wanted?

Enter Tumblr, a social media platform that marries traditional blogging functionality with an interactive social component. In looking at the social media efforts of peer institutions, we quickly realized that not only were a large number posting content on Tumblr, they were actively engaging with one another on the platform. Molly McArdle explores this phenomenon in her *Library Journal* article "The Library Is Open: A Look at Librarians and Tumblr," explaining that Tumblr has quickly become an ideal platform for libraries and archives—in part for its attractive, user-friendly, and media-rich interface, but especially for its social features (reblogging, tagging, commenting, and following), which encourage engagement, discovery, and community. Tumblr, she explains, is a "built-in community with built-in readers. . . . Once [librarians] arrived, they began to run into each other, then to talk with one another, and finally to understand themselves as a community."[8]

Encouraged by the success of peer institutions and by the potential community we might find, we switched the bulk of our social media activities to Tumblr in February 2014 and quickly found the engagement—and the community—we sought. The blogging feature at the core of Tumblr's platform allows us to be as brief or expansive as we'd like, from in-depth explorations of manuscript collections to informal GIFs of illustrations and photographs, and the social components—especially the keyword tagging and explore features—have helped us find and interact with other libraries and archives. What's more, the types of casual interaction Tumblr encourages— "Liking," commenting, reblogging—have loosened our tendency to be somewhat formal, and the friendlier, more approachable tone and tenor of our posts has in turn generated more engagement with our community.

Takeaways:

- Not all social media platforms are alike—if your current platform doesn't fit the type of interaction or communication you're looking for, don't be afraid to experiment until you find one that does.
- Engagement is the key to success—if you want to move beyond simple "Like" or "follow-back" behavior, find a platform that makes it easy to engage with others.

LOOKING AHEAD: FINAL THOUGHTS AND RECOMMENDATIONS

In our three years working first as an ad hoc group, then as a formal committee, and now as a larger community of contributors from different IS departments, we learned a lot through trial and error. Initially, our social media efforts were focused on unidirectional broadcasting, advertising events, services, and content to our community. Over time, we've come to understand the power of social media as a starting point for conversation. Now we use social media to listen to others, to post and talk about what they do, and to cultivate a diversity of content creators and posting types. Combining "listening" with "talking" is essential for us to get beyond the banality of marketing to a place where we can interact with, document, and build our community. We share information with our community and, in turn, learn about its needs, interests, and expectations.

Our social media activities have strengthened working relationships across departments in our division and enabled us to connect with other members of the college community in new, exciting, and meaningful ways. We have worked to cultivate a diverse group of contributors—students, staff, and faculty—and we recommend involving a wide variety of people in your efforts. The challenge is to make it easy for people to participate, to meet them where they are, and to bring them along at a speed with which they are comfortable.

We find that monthly meetings are important to maintain momentum and to support each other and our efforts. These meetings include any interested contributors across all departments in our division, including student workers, and provide opportunities to follow up on initiatives, brainstorm new ideas, and update each other on what is happening across the division. While we support individuality in social media efforts, these meetings provide focus, stability, and a collaborative space for content generation.

The Social Media Guide is a flexible tool that we recommend to any library to create and use. Because it is a living document, we reference it often, adding to and changing it as needed to reflect current trends in social media and adapt to our needs. It is not a panacea, however, and requires regular maintenance, reflection, and assessment to be useful.

Our challenges are ongoing and manifold. Despite the formalization of our efforts, we continue to struggle to make social media a planned, routine activity, rather than a reactionary event. The tension between bureaucratization of social media activities and the need to be flexible in order to follow our audience is ever present. Lack of time, resources, and administrative recognition of the work of creating, managing, and maintaining social media inhibits momentum. We nevertheless continue, buoyed by our successes and encouragement from our small community.

The only constant is change—this truism is particularly apt in the realm of social media. The dynamic nature of social media, with its ever-changing platforms and shifting allegiances among student users, is in tension with the stability that we may expect in our everyday work. In order to be successful, we've realized that we need not only to staff our channels but also to self-assess regularly and adapt accordingly. Seeking the ideal balance between routinization and innovation keeps us on our virtual toes.

NOTES

1. Nancy Dowd, "Social Media: Libraries Are Posting, but Is Anyone Listening?" *Library Journal* 138 (2013): 10–12.

2. "LITA Midwinter Workshops, 2014," last modified March 24, 2016, www.ala.org/lita/conferences/midwinter/2014.

3. Andrew Lopez, Rebecca Parmer, Jessica McCullough, and Laura Little, "Starting a New Twitter Account @ConnCollegeIS: With a Report from #ALAMW14," *Journal of Electronic Resources Librarianship* 26, no. 2 (2014): 150–52.

4. "Social Media Guide," Montana State University Library, accessed November 17, 2016, lib.montana.edu/about/social-media/guide.

5. "Information Services Social Media Policy," Connecticut College, accessed November 17, 2016, www.conncoll.edu/information-services/policies/is-social-media-policy/.

6. "#connfreespeech Twitter Hashtag Search Results," accessed February 13, 2017, twitter.com/search?q=%23connfreespeech&src=typd.

7. "Engage: Teaching with Technology at Connecticut College," Connecticut College, last modified February 10, 2017, teachtechconncoll.wordpress.com.

8. Molly McCardle, "The Library Is Open: A Look at Librarians and Tumblr," *Library Journal*, June 25, 2013, reviews.libraryjournal.com/2013/06/in-the-bookroom/post/the-library-is-open-a-look-at-librarians-and-tumblr/.

BIBLIOGRAPHY

"#connfreespeech Twitter Hashtag Search Results." Accessed February 13, 2017. twitter.com/search?q=%23connfreespeech&src=typd.

Dowd, Nancy. "Social Media: Libraries Are Posting, but Is Anyone Listening?" *Library Journal* 138 (2013): 10–12.

"Engage: Teaching with Technology at Connecticut College." Connecticut College. Last modified February 10, 2017. teachtechconncoll.wordpress.com.

"Information Services Social Media Policy." Connecticut College. Accessed November 17, 2016. www.conncoll.edu/information-services/policies/is-social-media-policy/.

"LITA Midwinter Workshops, 2014." Last modified March 24, 2016. www.ala.org/lita/conferences/midwinter/2014.

Lopez, Andrew, Rebecca Parmer, Jessica McCullough, and Laura Little. "Starting a New Twitter Account @ConnCollegeIS: With a Report from #ALAMW14." *Journal of Electronic Resources Librarianship* 26, no. 2 (2014): 150–52.

McCardle, Molly. "The Library Is Open: A Look at Librarians and Tumblr." *Library Journal*, June 25, 2013. reviews.libraryjournal.com/2013/06/in-the-bookroom/post/the-library-is-open-a-look-at-librarians-and-tumblr/.

"Social Media Guide." Montana State University Library. Accessed November 17, 2016. lib.montana.edu/about/social-media/guide.

3

Find Us on Facebook

The Evolution of Social Media at a Community College Library

Dana A. Knott and Angel M. Gondek

OVERVIEW

In the 1989 film *Field of Dreams*, Iowa farmer Ray Kinsella, played by Kevin Costner, hears a mysterious voice arise from his cornfields: "If you build it, he will come." After more whispers from his crops and a vision, Ray plows over the majority of his cornfields and builds a baseball diamond, a seemingly crazy move that threatens his ability to support his family. Yet the ghosts of baseball greats, including Shoeless Joe Jackson, appear to play ball. After going on a spiritual quest, during which he kidnaps reclusive writer Terence Mann, reminiscent of J. D. Salinger, and experiences other mystical occurrences, Ray reunites with his deceased father for a game of catch, fulfilling the prophecy. Terence Mann predicts, "People will come, Ray," and a long line of cars travels to Ray's baseball diamond to pay for the privilege to watch the ultimate ball game. Ray mends his broken relationship with his father and saves the family farm in the process.

The film's original quote has morphed into "If you build it, *they* will come" and continues to remain a part of our popular culture to this day. The quote hints that even a small effort or investment can lead to success and a big payout. So what does this quote have to do with libraries and social media? Libraries that take the first steps to create social media accounts, from Facebook to Instagram, may quickly discover that it is not enough to "build it," that joining social media does not immediately result in a large number of likes and followers, although it represents a step in the right direction. Sadly, it is not that easy. Cultivating relationships online takes a lot of planning and work. When the Columbus State Library joined the ranks of libraries on social media, our Social Media Team identified the purpose: "to enhance the Library's social media presence and identify opportunities to utilize social media tools (Facebook, YouTube, Instagram, Twitter, Flickr, Tumblr, etc.) to communicate and interact with Columbus State Community College students, faculty, staff, partners, and the surrounding community." But how does a library enhance its online presence and cultivate relationships? Since our library took those initial steps by joining social media platforms, our approach to social media has evolved and key library events contributed to this evolution.

SOCIAL MEDIA BEGINNINGS

The Columbus State Library did not always have as vibrant a presence on social media, and it wasn't until 2011 that the library acknowledged its need to establish a presence over social media and connect with its community online, especially since Columbus State Community College offers a robust distance learning program. Indeed, establishing and maintaining a vibrant social media presence can present a challenge for community college libraries. Some of these libraries may not have their own marketing department and must rely on staff who take on the task of posting or tweeting in addition to their main responsibilities. Any reluctance to take on additional duties must give way to the opportunities social media offers to libraries to build meaningful connections online. In its inception, the library's social media efforts were tasked to one full-time staff member, but as additional social networking opportunities presented themselves, it became apparent that staff needed to be added in order to create unique content across platforms. As a small library, we also did not have the ability to hire a staff member solely dedicated to social media and marketing. With the creation of a Social Media Team, our library took a divide-and-conquer approach to social media, and five librarians focused on different platforms: Facebook, Twitter, Instagram, Tumblr, and Pinterest. Fortunately, the library Social Media Team did not need to start from scratch when developing social media guidelines; instead, it built on the college's best practices, which advised staff to follow established brand standards, identify backup administrators, respect privacy and uphold confidentiality, and thoroughly understand social media platforms and communities (www.cscc.edu/_resources/media/about/pdf/Social%20media%20guidelines.pdf). Important best practices also included "Think twice and re-read before posting," "Be transparent," and "Post regularly/consistently." These practices sound deceptively obvious, but such commonsense advice can quickly fall to the wayside when other library tasks take precedence over posting regularly to the library's Facebook page. Our library was fortunate to be a part of an institution that encourages departments to reach out to their communities through social media. Based on our experience, libraries should familiarize themselves with their institution's social media guidelines before taking the plunge into library participation in social media.

Initially, the library utilized social media as a marketing tool to share information about the library, its services and workshops, and important semester reminders for students. Team responsibilities centered on the promotional aspects of social media, and posts predominately focused on the library as a brand and library links; however, the library began to realize that social media can be a powerful relationship builder when the library began planning its first Banned Books Week celebration for 2014. Social media as a promotional tool represents only one part of the equation. The library cannot ignore the need to nurture online relationships, connections, and positive associations.

In May 2014, the Freedom to Read Foundation awarded the Columbus State Library its Judith Krug Fund Banned Books Week Events Grant. In our proposal, our library emphasized the role that social media would play in our Banned Books Week programming, and this focus on social media appealed to the Freedom to Read Foundation. As a community college library with a diverse student population that does not live on campus, our library identified social media as the best means to reach our students, those who took traditional, face-to-face classes and those who took online classes. Social media can create meaningful connections between people and their libraries. With that in mind, social media played a starring role in the library's Banned Books Week programming. Our library desired to provide various opportunities for our community members to contribute to an online exhibit that celebrates intellectual freedom and access to information. Social media offered a powerful vehicle for participants to curate their own experiences and add their voices to the conversation. With our theme of "Exhibit the Right to Read," and strong emphasis on the word "Exhibit," our library offered a story-recording booth and a "mug shot" photo booth; recordings and images were then archived on a WordPress site specifically created for the celebration (library.cscc.edu/exhibit). More traditional Banned Books Week activities, such as a poetry reading, were paired with online components. Exhibit the Right to Read events employed a multitude of social media tools to contact a variety of users with a variety of different social media preferences. Our library's Social Media Team coordinated efforts to avoid replication. Student interactions with the library over social media were rewarded with entries in our Banned Books Week raffle. The Exhibit the Right to Read events for Banned Books Week provided our library with opportunities to increase our interactions with our current social media accounts, such as Facebook and Twitter, and explore new social media platforms, such as Playbuzz and BuzzFeed.

EXPERIMENTING WITH SOCIAL MEDIA

Pokémon Go

While libraries certainly should use social media platforms to highlight programs and services, libraries need to remember that social media can be an effective tool to build relationships. These relationship-building posts are not necessarily those that even mention library services; instead, posts that tap into community interests can go a long way in cultivating relationships. Our library more fully appreciated this approach when the Pokémon Go craze began the summer of 2016. #CSCCLibraryPokemon and #catchthemall became popular hashtags on the Columbus State Library's social media platforms, such as Instagram and Twitter. Pokémon Go is a free mobile app that allows "trainers" to hunt for and capture Pokémon, some elusive, with the goal to "catch them all." Pokémon Go incorporates augmented reality and a smartphone's GPS to seek Pokémon. The Columbus State Library is a Pokémon Go "gym" where teams Mystic, Valor, and Instinct can train their Pokémon and battle rivals to become the gym leader. Columbus State's campus also has several "Pokéstops," such as its Christopher Columbus statue, where trainers can refill Poké balls used to capture Pokémon and other items.

Between classes, groups of students gathered at the library, furiously tapping their smartphones as they battled Pokémon from opposing teams to win the gym. Many library staff members were Pokémon trainers themselves and quickly identified an opportunity to connect with students through Pokémon Go, and social media provided the perfect vehicle to enhance our library's relationship with our community through a shared love for Pokémon. Indeed, an Instagram post showing that Pokémon Go buttons (see figure 3.1) were available at the Circulation Desk was one of the library's most popular, and buttons quickly disappeared as the news spread that our library had cool Pokémon buttons, such as "I survived a Pokémon Go battle at the Columbus State Library and all I got was this button."

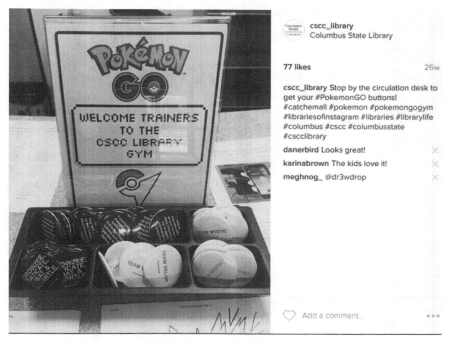

Figure 3.1.   Pokémon Go buttons

Social media also allowed our library to have fun, Pokémon-related interactions with our community. For example, our library hid 3D-printed Pokémon in our library and around our Columbus and Delaware campuses and encouraged students who found a Pokémon to share a picture and tag the library on social media (see figure 3.2).

Sure enough, lucky students shared their finds over Instagram and tagged the library, and a student visited the reference desk to have a librarian snap a picture of her 3D-printed Pokémon and upload it to social media for her. Faculty even contacted the library to ask about Pokémon and how to incorporate the game into their classes.

Our library was not alone in using Pokémon Go as a relationship builder and to generate a little bit of fun. Businesses, from coffee shops to zoos, advertised themselves as gyms or Pokéstops to bring in more customers. Libraries also were quick to surf the Pokémon Go wave. For fun, our library created a "Pokémon Go! A Cultural Phenomenon: @CSCC" guide with information about the game and a map of the various Pokéstops on the Columbus and Delaware campuses (library.cscc.edu/pokemongo). Other libraries published their own Pokémon Go guides, including University of Nebraska–Omaha's "Pokémon Go at UNO" and Florida International University's "PokéGuide: Pokémon Go @FIULibraries." Reddit's r/Libraries community contained numerous posts on libraries jumping on the Pokémon Go bandwagon, and librarians even created a Facebook group for Library Pokémon Go Support and #PokeLibrary to share ideas on Pokémon-related programming. If librarians were unaware of the Pokémon Go phenomenon, numerous librarian publications were sure to encourage them to join the movement. Fortunately, we librarians live in a time where ideas are readily shared online. The Pokémon Go phenomenon offered our library and many other libraries an entertaining opportunity to forge new

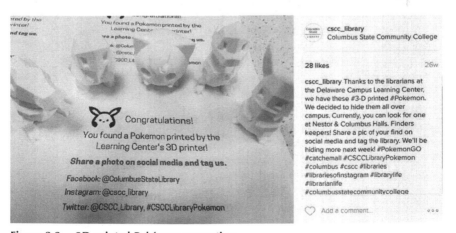

Figure 3.2.   3D-printed Pokémon promotion

relationships. Librarians should acknowledge that their relationships with librarians and other libraries can provide inspiration and contribute to relationship building.

Playbuzz

Perhaps the most popular and impactful use of social media for our Exhibit the Right to Read programming was the "Which Banned Book Are You?" online quiz. Our library wanted to tap into the popularity of online quizzes and share the quiz over different social media platforms, including Twitter and Facebook. When one thinks about personality quizzes, BuzzFeed immediately comes to mind; however, at the time, BuzzFeed did not allow users to create and share online quizzes through its site, so our library opted for BuzzFeed competitor Playbuzz as an alternative. Playbuzz identifies itself as "a digital publishing platform that empowers publishers, marketers, bloggers and brands to easily create content using media formats that are optimized for social sharing and engagement."[1] It provides users and libraries with the tools required to readily create and publish their own content, including interactive personality quizzes, and share content across different platforms. The "Which Banned Book Are You?" quiz asks users familiar questions, such as their favorite board game, food, and song, and then matches them to their banned book personality. For example, *The Hunger Games* was a possible result and it was accompanied with the personality description "You would do anything to protect the ones you love and would volunteer as Tribute any time. Even if you don't know how to shoot a bow and arrow, your aim is true when it comes to picking out a good dystopian novel to read." The quiz's popularity went well beyond the library's expectations, with more than 329,000 shares. The American Library Association even issued a press release, "Quiz Promotes Banned Books Week, Sept. 21-27," that highlighted the Columbus State Library's "Which Banned Book Are You?" online quiz (www.ala.org/news/press-releases/2014/09/quiz-promotes-banned-books-week-sept-21-27). It amazed us that a simple quiz could resonate with so many people beyond our college community, and the quiz certainly underscores the impact that social media can have. Our library continues to use Playbuzz to create personality quizzes for Banned Books Week and for National Poetry Month with the "Who Is Your Inner Poet?" quiz. For the Olympics, our library posted a "Which Olympic Sport Should You Play?" quiz to highlight an event trending in the news. Personality quizzes are fun and addictive and offer a popular and interactive means for readers' advisory. While the Columbus State Library limits Playbuzz to the library's big events throughout the year due to time constraints and work responsibilities, any library should consider how it can use Playbuzz as a promotional or educational tool.

Libraries can sign up for a free Playbuzz account and brand their "channel" with a logo, cover image, and public profile. They can also add a Facebook page plug-in and a Twitter feed plug-in to connect their channel to other social media platforms. Quiz takers then can post their quiz results and share the quizzes with their Facebook friends or use Twitter to retweet their results. In addition to personality quizzes, librarians can use Playbuzz to create video snaps, lists, countdowns, and polls. Creating quizzes in Playbuzz is fairly straightforward. When our library began developing its "Which Banned Book Are You?" quiz, we found it easiest to first identify the results, in this instance eight commonly banned books, and then customize questions and images to the results. While Playbuzz encourages its users to provide attribution for images, our library selected images from the public domain, such as those from MorgueFile and Wikimedia Commons. Answers can also be weighted to refer to more than one result. While it can be time consuming to map out the quiz, write up witty result descriptions, and select images, the final result is well worth the necessary effort it takes to publish a personality quiz.

In 2016, Playbuzz added an "Impact" feature, previously in beta, that allows a channel to track its views, start rate, completion rate, and social interaction for each quiz or list. Playbuzz calls Impact a "personal roadmap to engagement."[2] Now libraries using Playbuzz will have a clearer picture of what appeals to their community and the reach they may have. According to Playbuzz Impact, the "Which Olympic Sport Should You Play?" quiz achieved almost seventeen thousand views in under a week. It is one thing for a library to create a quiz and put it out there; it is quite another thing for a library to assess the reach and impact of its content. Views do have value, but libraries can use completion rate data to reexamine content or better define what signifies a successful interaction. If a user stopped taking a quiz at a certain question, the library can go back into the quiz and revise. Analytic features, such as Impact, serve as a social media librarian's ally. Librarians should not remain content in merely posting but should also mindfully think about what garners a strong response and why and identify areas for improvement.

BuzzFeed

Playbuzz rival BuzzFeed describes itself as "a cross-platform, global network for news and entertainment that generates seven billion views each month. BuzzFeed creates and distributes content for a global audience and utilizes proprietary technology to continuously test, learn and optimize." Initially recognized for its viral content and, in particular, its personality quizzes, BuzzFeed has strived in recent years to publish digital news produced by its own investigative news journalists. Many librarians on the Social Media Team were already familiar with BuzzFeed's personality quizzes and viral content with titles that demand a click. In 2014, when our library first considered BuzzFeed as a social media tool for its Banned Books Week campaign, BuzzFeed offered a Community Brand Publisher platform, which allowed institutions, including libraries, to create accounts and brand content for free.

In addition to its personality quizzes, BuzzFeed's listicles remain popular. A listicle, as the name suggests, is a numbered list with a catchy title, centered around a theme, and made more magnetic through the inclusion of images or GIFs. Recent BuzzFeed listicles include "22 Libraries That Will Give You Serious Reading Goals" and "19 Heartbreaking 'Harry Potter' Tumblr Posts That Will Make You Cry." Since Banned

Books Week 2014 focused on graphic novels, the Columbus State Library published a listicle titled "20 Life Lessons Learned from Reading Banned and Challenged Comics," which includes such life lessons as "Fight for all that is pre-shrunk and cottony" for the oft-challenged *The Adventures of Captain Underpants*. A significant downside, however, involved the inability to search for lists created by community accounts. Community listicles become searchable only if showcased by BuzzFeed's editors; as a result, our library relied on Facebook and Twitter to share a direct link to the listicle. BuzzFeed allows site visitors to post their reactions with "badges" that include hearts and SMS (texting) language, including OMG, LOL, and EW. Community accounts can even earn BuzzFeed awards for click-worthy, online masterpieces. Facebook conversations also showcase social media reactions below the post and encourage additional online interactions. BuzzFeed provides analytics for its community accounts to track interactions, and according to BuzzFeed statistics, the library's listicle had a total of 3,756 views during Banned Books Week. In a case of bad timing for the library, BuzzFeed finally gave its community accounts the ability to create personality quizzes just after Banned Books Week.

Even with the newly granted ability to create personality quizzes in addition to more listicles, our library had little opportunity to explore how it could best utilize BuzzFeed as a social media tool. In March of 2015, BuzzFeed froze its Community Brand Publisher accounts with the statement, "If you are an organization, a brand, or an individual with a political or commercial agenda, BuzzFeed's Community platform is probably not the best place for you." As a non-profit educational institution, our library does not have a political nor a commercial agenda, and we even contacted BuzzFeed to discuss our account, although our e-mail did not receive a response. Despite the frozen account, the library's listicle remains accessible online as evidence of the one piece of online content the library published through BuzzFeed. With its BuzzFeed Community Brand Publisher account frozen, our library decided to continue to use Playbuzz to create and publish its digital content, from quizzes to lists.

Other libraries can certainly find inspiration from BuzzFeed's personality quizzes. For example, the University of California–Merced Library developed a BuzzFeed-inspired quiz to connect to students during their "Bobcat Day" orientation. Their personality quiz results matched students to specific spaces in their library, such as their collaborative work rooms or quiet reading rooms. Their personality quiz offered a more engaging means to introduce students to the library. With such a positive student response, the University of California–Merced librarians "encourage other libraries to consider creating similar activities in order to generate dialogue about services, spaces, and research at their campuses."[3] While the UC–Merced librarians opted for a paper format for their BuzzFeed-inspired quiz, other librarians can certainly utilize social media tools to introduce students to library resources in a fun way. Although BuzzFeed put the kibosh on Community Brand Publisher accounts, individual librarians can sign up for a BuzzFeed community account with their Facebook, Twitter, or Google+ account to begin creating content, but they still must rely on BuzzFeed editors to feature their creations in the hopes of reaching viral status. Of course, they can, like the Columbus State Library, select Playbuzz as an alternative.

Libraries need not have a BuzzFeed account to employ BuzzFeed in their information literacy programs. Carroll University librarian Joe Hardenbrook, known for his Mr. Library Dude blog (mrlibrarydude.wordpress.com), has students in his information literacy sessions, which are specifically customized for introduction to psychology courses, examine a news article related to psychology from BuzzFeed news, an article posted to Facebook, and another article from *Huffington Post*. Working in separate groups, students examine their article to identify the original sources of information mentioned in the source. From the BuzzFeed article, the students noted that it cited a study detailed in the *New York Times*. The students then went to the *New York Times* article, which identified the researcher's name and a scholarly article that they were able to access through their own library's databases. Such an activity underscores that while students can begin their research with Google or locate information from social media, they must follow the information trail to more scholarly resources, which they then may search for in research databases. Hardenbrook notes, "Every day we read, see, or hear about things that involve academic research—on almost any topic imaginable. We just have to do a little digging to get to that research."[4] User-created content remains the heart of BuzzFeed, and quizzes, including "Which 'Little Mermaid' Character Are You Based on Your Seafood Preferences?," continue to reel in visitors with click-bait titles; however, BuzzFeed has worked hard in recent years to publish more serious, news-related content. Will librarians now consider BuzzFeed news on par with more established news sources such as the *Washington Post* or the *New York Times*? Perhaps students in information literacy classes can help answer that question.

LEGACY SOCIAL MEDIA EFFORTS, REVISITED

Twitter and Facebook

In all honesty, our library selected Twitter as its first social media account because it was a platform that many of the librarians were familiar with and comfortable using. Twitter lends itself readily to conversations in a fast-paced online environment. Our library could add to the conversation with a tweet or become a part of a larger conversation and community by retweeting a tweet from another user. During its Banned Books Week celebrations, our library tweeted information about its programs, but more importantly, its tweets encouraged dialogue and reflection on important themes, including the freedom of ideas and diversity. Our library uses the more "grandfatherly" Facebook as a more traditional marketing tool to promote events, resources, and information, though in recent years, library Facebook posts may struggle to achieve a higher organic reach without paying for a "boost."[5] In June 2016, Facebook changed its News Feed algorithm, so that the posts appearing on an individual's News Feed are now more selective and relevant. As a result, a library page's organic reach may decline. According to Facebook's engineering director, Lars Backstrom, "If a lot of your referral traffic is the result of people sharing your content and their friends liking and commenting on it, there will be less of an impact than if the majority of your traffic comes directly through Page posts. We encourage Pages to post things that their audience are likely to share with their friends."[6] Now more than ever, libraries must discover content that resonates with their audience, posts considered "share-worthy." Before such changes, our library predominantly relied on Facebook and Twitter for our Banned Books Week campaign. At the end of Banned Books Week, our library gained more than 6,600 impressions through Twitter, 97 mentions, 1,144 engagements and 17 new followers over Facebook, and 881 views of Banned Books Week videos on the library's YouTube channel. As a Twitter metric, impressions can help libraries gauge the potential reach of a tweet. Utilizing Twitter metrics also allows content creators to determine the best time to tweet to their audience and what types of tweets garner the most attention. This is valuable information to assist in creating an effective message in a limited format.

Twitter provides its own metrics through the Twitter Analytics site, www.ana lyticstwitter.com. Twitter users can view granular usage statistics regarding their account, including tweets that garnered the highest impressions, the number of mentions a post has, and who the top followers are. From the data gathered throughout Banned Books Week, the Columbus State Library noticed that tweets that connected directly with other users in dialogue or shared promotion helped boost organic outreach through "likes" and "retweets." Analytics can also provide insight into the type of content that users prefer. These types of statistics have shown that tweets containing links to additional content or multimedia messages are more engaging than basic statements or questions. In this sense, Twitter as a platform is more about creating a conversation, and keeping it going, than mere promotion.

Facebook, on the other hand, serves as an almost instantaneous promotional platform. Content creators don't need to spend as much time curating their friends list to ensure that they are following other organizations that will share their content. Instead it is a platform designed to directly display information to an audience of willing participants. Creators have the freedom to post a variety of ways, without the 140-character constraint of Twitter. That's not to say that Facebook doesn't have a downside in terms of reaching its intended audience. Many users have complained that Facebook's algorithm is biased against organizations and businesses, often making it difficult for information to spread in a timely manner. Facebook data is not an exact science; a post might have reached more than a thousand users, but that number reflects the number of Facebook feeds in which a post was displayed. It does not reflect whether the user was engaged or read the post. While some organizations have turned to paying to boost posts, it is still unclear as to whether this expense has beneficial return on investment (ROI).

Pinterest

Images centered around a specific theme lie at the heart of Pinterest. Pinterest aptly identifies itself as "the world's catalog of an idea," a description that certainly speaks to librarians. With Pinterest, a library can easily create a profile with its own branding and create boards that showcase new items in a library's collection, contain pictures from library events, or provide pins of online resources. Libraries can even use their Facebook account to log into Pinterest or link their Pinterest account to Facebook or Twitter, which would allow libraries to quickly share a board or a pin over various platforms. For its Exhibit the Right to Read Campaign, our library created a board on "Banned and Challenged Graphic Novels and Comics" and another board representative of an online "Banned Books Week Film Festival." Early in the Banned Books Week planning process, our library considered having a film festival showcasing films based on banned or challenged novels; when the cost of purchasing public performance rights to show films proved too prohibitive, Pinterest offered a free means to highlight films by pinning trailers and film clips from YouTube. With its Banned Books Week–themed boards, the library reached 2,385 users and had 4,154 impressions and 22 repins. Pinterest impressions represent "the number of times a Pin from your profile has appeared on *Pinterest* home feeds, category feeds and search." In addition to its Banned Books Week–related boards, the library published boards on iPad apps for college students, National Poetry Month, recipes for culinary students, and even a board with Bigfoot pins to supplement an outreach program to fourth graders that uses Bigfoot to teach information literacy. Another bonus of Pinterest is its ability to connect with other apps. For example, users can pin their Instagram photos to a Pinterest board or even pin their favorite handmade crafts from Etsy.

While libraries have used Pinterest boards to highlight gems from their collections, whether physical or digital, more libraries have begun to explore how Pinterest can play a role in information literacy sessions, a social media tool that also can serve as a teaching tool. Central Methodist University has integrated Pinterest in its info lit sessions for beginning composition classes. Students set up their own Pinterest accounts and create a board to which they pin relevant images representative of a key concept: "Incorporating activities utilizing Pinterest has not only afforded opportunity to create engaging assignments but also provided opportunities for student[s] to develop transliteracy skills."[7] Pinterest allows students to think critically about gathering and evaluating resources in a dynamic and visual way.

With emphasis on the dynamic and the visual, the library avoids lengthy lists of books from its catalog or online resources in its LibGuides by including Pinterest boards, such as the library's LGBT board, to supplement the research guides and lead students to additional resources.

Instagram

Purchased by Facebook in 2012, Instagram is a mobile-based social media app that allows users to share artfully composed pictures of latte art and hearts drawn in the sand. In all seriousness, though, Instagram offers librarians the ability to share visually dynamic images and videos with their followers. Libraries may use an e-mail or a Facebook account to sign up for Instagram, and librarians who have their own personal account can add their library's account and easily toggle between the two. While librarians may use a computer to sign up for an Instagram account and view photos, they can upload and share pictures and videos only through the mobile app. Technology-shy librarians may desire a web-based version of Instagram, but Instagram's mobile app readily allows for librarians to snap and share a picture, as the name implies, in an instant. Librarians can even upload a short video of up to sixty seconds. Instagram also offers different photo filters, such as Inkwell, Lo-Fi, and Juno, to suggest a certain mood or go retro, which might be fun for #tbt (Throwback Thursday) or #fbf (Flashback Friday) postings. The cool visuals speak louder than words, and Instagram offers native apps, apps created for a specific platform, such as Layouts for Instagram and Boomerang for Instagram, to offer users more freedom to enhance their uploads beyond filters. Layout allows users to create a collage of images with the option of adding borders. Essentially Boomerang is a Graphics Interchange Format (GIF) maker that records a short video and loops it for fun results. It works well to add more visual variety to one's Instagram feed. Libraries can also download the Gifshare app, which offers more editing options and the ability to convert a GIF to a video to post to Instagram.

Instead of lengthy descriptions, librarians can use hashtags with a limit of thirty hashtags per post, though it's for the best not to get too crazy with the hashtags even when they can lead to new users who discovered your account. When users tap on an Instagram hashtag, they are taken to a page of items that include content under that hashtag. Our library has connected to other libraries with the hashtags #librariesofinstagram, #librarylife, and #humansofthelibrary. As our library has amassed followers, it has also followed other libraries and its own followers to strengthen further online relationships and to generate ideas from other captivating posts. The library's Instagram account has its obligatory shelfies, pictures of bookshelves that have become popular on Instagram, and even presented a summer Dewey Decimal tour showcasing different titles on the shelf. Yet librarians must remember to include posts in their Instagram feed that highlight the human faces of the library. Not only does our library include staff introductions but photos of students with information about their college goals and what they like best about their library. The University of Montevallo Library in Alabama uses Instagram for its library orientation program, during which students can take shelfies and selfies that introduce both resources and the people of the library. Students are sent throughout the library to upload and caption pictures of "the weirdest book in the reference section," "the best study spot," and a selfie with a library staff member.[8] In addition to posting their images to the library's Instagram feed, students were encouraged to share their feelings and experiences in their captions in the more comfortable and less rigid environment social media offers. Success often lies in creating experiences and stories. How do libraries share their stories and also allow their communities to add to the narrative?

Introduced in August 2016, Instagram Stories, strongly reminiscent of Snapchat Stories, allows librarians to share more personal aspects about their libraries and communities without overloading their feeds. In addition to the Instagram filters, users can add text and drawings to add even more visual appeal. Instagram stories, which appear at the top of a feed, last for only twenty-four hours. For National Book Lovers Day, our library shared an Instagram story in which people shared their favorite books. One does not need to be Steven Spielberg to post a short video to Instagram Stories. The beauty arises from a story's less polished and more natural narrative. Our library plans on offering more Instagram stories throughout the year for different college and national events and theme days with the hope that these stories will contribute to deeper interactions. In August 2014, before our inaugural Banned Books Week celebration, our library had only forty-four followers on Instagram. That number was well over five hundred in early October 2016, largely in part to targeted interactions, increased use of tagging and hashtagging, and engagement incentives.

In addition to Instagram Stories, Instagram unveiled Instagram for Business. Libraries with an Instagram account can easily convert to a business account by going to settings and selecting "Switch to Business Profile." This switch will bring access to Instagram's business tools, such as "insights" into post performance and follower demographics, including age. Insight metrics detail impressions, reach, and engagement and organize posts based on number of impressions. Business profiles will allow libraries to add more contact information to their profiles and even promote their posts. The "promote" feature will require a library with an Instagram business profile to connect its Facebook page to its Instagram account to create ads with Facebook's Ads Manager, which helps users design campaigns that focus on the following marketing objectives: awareness, consideration, and conversion. Some features of the business profile are free, but ads will require businesses to decide on how much to spend on paid advertisements. Does a switch to an Instagram business profile represent a smart marketing move or a move to the dark side? Presently, our library has taken a wait-and-see approach to Instagram for Business as it is a new product still being refined. More importantly, our hesitation arises from what drew our library to Instagram in the first place, the ability to gain followers organically with an app known for its beautiful simplicity and visuals. Paid ads, strategic and practical, threaten organic relationships and sincere engagement and may paint content as more predatory and less soulful.

BUILDING COLLABORATIONS AND CAPACITY

In the years since the Columbus State Library created its Twitter account in 2011, the library predominantly flew solo in its social media endeavors with the occasional cross-promotion of events. However, as the saying goes, no man is an island. No library should be an island, isolated or insular. In the summer of 2016, Columbus

State Community College developed a Social Media Engagement Plan with the main goals of using social media to effectively engage students and encourage collaboration. The Social Media Engagement Plan also resulted in the formation of a college-wide social media team with twenty members from various college departments, including the library, and that is overseen by the college's marketing coordinator. The team also includes social media student ambassadors who have their fingers on the pulse of what appeals to their fellow students. The Social Media Engagement Team currently focuses on using various social media platforms to connect to students, emphasize student success, and raise awareness of campus events and resources. A shared calendar also provides directions and encourages strategically timed posts and cross-pollination. As part of a vibrant educational institution, libraries must engage in what others are doing as part of a larger community.

The Social Media Engagement Team meets weekly to coordinate efforts between departments, cross-promote events, and convey a unified message. For the college's Week of Welcome, the team created the central hashtag #outofthegatecsstate. The team found inspiration from the Parkway School District in St. Louis, which asked its students to answer the question, "What is your hope?" For each day of Week of Welcome, the Social Media Engagement Team came up with a question partnered with a relevant hashtag:

- Monday: What's your talent? Post a photo, share a video, or use words to describe your skills so we can bow to your awesomeness. #cshastalent
- Tuesday: What #randomactofkindness have you done today? #csserviceonthego
- Wednesday: It's #WisdomWednesdsay. Hey, returning students, what advice do you have for new CSCC counterparts? (Tag @cscc_edu in your posts!)
- Thursday: Make a new friend. Take a selfie. #strangerselfiecscc

Social media ambassadors further promoted daily themes, snapped selfies with new students, and recorded videos of the campus's energetic first week of the fall semester. Before they set out on social media tasks, the ambassadors receive training about social media standards and expectations; ambassadors also must sign a social media contract.

Our library quickly reaped the benefits from this cross-campus collaboration. For Banned Books Week 2016, which focused on the theme of diversity, the Columbus State Library hosted a Human Library, and the enthusiasm and creativity of the social media ambassadors greatly enhanced the event. The Human Library grew from an international project first established in Copenhagen with the aim of breaking down stereotypes and fostering dialogue. Instead of books, the Human Library circulates human beings, who graciously share their lives, experiences, and stories with readers. The Columbus State Human Library books included women from the non-profit organization TransOhio that serves Ohio's transgender community, an African American poet and librarian, a woman who grew up in foster care, a man living with a traumatic brain injury, a daughter of immigrants, and a police officer.

A WordPress site (cscchumanlibrary.wordpress.com) served as an information hub and showcased the human books and story booth recordings. The Human Library included an iPad photo booth with a selfie picture frame branded with "The CSCC Human Library" and "Don't judge a book by its cover." The Simple Booth app allowed picture takers to e-mail themselves their photo strips and to share over Twitter or Facebook. Throughout the duration of the Human Library, social media ambassadors captured "snaps," ten-second videos recorded using the mobile app Snapchat, a social media platform very popular with a younger demographic. The ambassadors then compiled snaps to form a story to share over the college's Snapchat account; Snapchatters can view a story multiple times in a twenty-four-hour period. In addition to creating Snapchat stories to showcase different books and their conversations, the social media ambassadors recorded snaps of event visitors answering the question, "If you were a book, what would your title be in one word?" Before the Human Library, the ambassadors asked students across campus this question to promote the event and build a sense of involvement. The library currently does not have its own Snapchat account, but the social media ambassadors' cool snaps and Snapchat stories proved fun and inspirational. The social media student ambassadors even use their social media skills to promote smaller events. For example a social media student ambassador dropped by the library's 3D printing workshop at Columbus State's Delaware Campus and created an Instagram story that showcased our library's 3D printer and cool designs made by students. Librarians can definitely learn from our more social-media-savvy students and should consider having social media takeovers, such as by library student workers. Columbus State's social media ambassadors also teach courses to teachers and staff interested in learning more about social media to reach out to students. Really, there's no one better to teach about social media than a student active online.

FINAL THOUGHTS AND RECOMMENDATIONS

Our library has come a long way in its social media endeavors, yet the learning process continues. Successful forays into the realm of social media require diligence, reflection, and, importantly, teamwork. Consider the formation of a social media team for your library, one that highlights the strengths of its different members, yet doesn't limit membership to "Library Only." Instead, reach out to your institution's marketing and communications wings and other departments. A college-wide team allows for additional brainstorming and inspiration, cross-pollination, and a unified vision. Our library's participation in the college's Social Media Engagement Team has proved beneficial and has offered an additional layer of support along with the experience and knowledge of other members with strong marketing backgrounds. Weekly meetings ensure that our library's voice is heard and that other parts of our institution work with us in promoting our library. For your social media team, don't forget to recruit student workers to serve as social media ambassadors and provide an insider view. Their energy and enthusiasm are infectious. They can more comfortably approach their fellow students to capture a snap or an Instagram story.

Our library matched Social Media Team members with different social media platforms according to comfort level and experience. Think about how your library can also match your social media platforms with different goals. Our library tends to use Facebook for promotions, Twitter for generating conversations, and Instagram for emotional connections and storytelling. Developing best practices will guide and inform how your library utilizes each platform with professionalism and mindfulness at the center of each post or tweet. While creating social media guidelines or best practices, touch base with your marketing and communications department, an important step as representatives of not just your library but your institution. Don't forget to review best practices; social media platforms are not static, so your best practices cannot remain static.

Not many libraries have the monetary means to "boost" posts and increase reach. For Facebook, in particular, a budget can significantly increase reach; however, libraries with no budget must rely on more organic means to gain followers and connect online, which can be difficult with Facebook, a platform that has not been kind to non-profit organizations. As a start, though, follow and like institutional partners, fellow libraries, local businesses and community groups, and your own community members. Relationships with partner institutions over social media can be mutually beneficial. Go beyond likes: share or retweet and don't forget to respond to build those relationships and emphasize the human element.

Our library's social media successes often arose from campaigns that targeted important events. Big events, such as the library's annual Banned Books Week celebration, can serve as a much needed catalyst to spur greater creativity and activity online to augment online relationships and ignite positive vibes between students and their libraries. Yet libraries must not forget the quieter moments between events. Those quieter moments offer opportunities to share a story, capture an experience, and show value. It's easy to post about an upcoming library workshop; it's much more difficult to impart worth or generate further a positive response to the library as a brand with real, caring people available to help the members of its community to achieve success.

NOTES

1. "About Playbuzz," Playbuzz, accessed February 13, 2017, playbuzz.fanbread.com/about.

2. "Playbuzz Impact," Playbuzz, accessed February 13, 2017, publishers.playbuzz.com/academy/how_to/playbuzz-impact.

3. Elizabeth McMunn-Tetangco, "Where (in the Library) Do You Belong? Using an Informal Quiz to Engage Prospective New Students," *College & Research Libraries News* 76, no. 11 (2015): 582–85.

4. Joe Hardenbrook, "BuzzFeed & Facebook in Infolit Sessions: Connecting What Students Use to Library Research," Mr. Library Dude (blog), February 25, 2015, mrlibrarydude.

wordpress.com/2015/02/25/buzzfeed-facebook-in-infolit-sessions-connecting-what-students-use-to-library-research.

5. See chapter 5 in this book for more information on Facebook advertising.

6. Lars Backstrom, "News Feed FYI: Helping Make Sure You Don't Miss Stories from Friends," Facebook Newsroom (blog), June 29, 2016, newsroom.fb.com/news/2016/06/news-feed-fyi-helping-make-sure-you-dont-miss-stories-from-friends/.

7. Cynthia Dundenhoffer, "Visualizing Information with Pinterest," in *Using Social Media in Libraries*, ed. Charles Harmon and Michael Messina (Lanham, MD: Scarecrow Press, 2013), 30.

8. Lauren Wallis, "#selfiesinthestacks: Sharing the Library with Instagram," *Internet Reference Services Quarterly* 19 (2014): 181–206.

BIBLIOGRAPHY

"About Playbuzz." Playbuzz. Accessed February 13, 2017. playbuzz.fanbread.com/about.

Backstrom, Lars. "News Feed FYI: Helping Make Sure You Don't Miss Stories from Friends." Facebook Newsroom (blog), June 29, 2016, newsroom.fb.com/news/2016/06/news-feed-fyi-helping-make-sure-you-dont-miss-stories-from-friends/.

Dundenhoffer, Cynthia. "Visualizing Information with Pinterest." In *Using Social Media in Libraries*, edited by Charles Harmon and Michael Messina, 23–36. Lanham, MD: Scarecrow Press, 2013.

Hardenbrook, Joe. "BuzzFeed & Facebook in Infolit Sessions: Connecting What Students Use to Library Research." Mr. Library Dude (blog), February 25, 2015, mrlibrarydude.wordpress.com/2015/02/25/buzzfeed-facebook-in-infolit-sessions-connecting-what-students-use-to-library-research/.

McMunn-Tetangco, Elizabeth. "Where (in the Library) Do You Belong? Using an Informal Quiz to Engage Prospective New Students." *College & Research Libraries News* 76, no. 11 (2015): 582–85.

"Playbuzz Impact." Playbuzz. Accessed February 13, 2017, publishers.playbuzz.com/academy/how_to/playbuzz-impact.

Wallis, Lauren. "#selfiesinthestacks: Sharing the Library with Instagram." *Internet Reference Services Quarterly* 19 (2014): 181–206.

4

Social Media and Health Care

Building and Sustaining Communities for Patients and Providers

Patricia J. Devine

OVERVIEW

The use of social media to keep up with rapidly changing technologies and advances in the field of medicine is growing among Americans. The use of the Internet to find health information has increased steadily over the past several years. According to the Pew Research Center, 87 percent of adults in the United States used the Internet as of January 2014, and 72 percent of those users looked for health information online within the previous year.[1] One in four adults who use the Internet search online for information about their own or someone else's medical issue, and 16 percent have used the Internet to find others who share their health concerns.[2] While most people still turn to clinicians for information about their health, increasingly health-care consumers seek others who have similar conditions to talk to, seek advice from, and create bonds with. This subsequent sense of community, whether online or in person, leads to more engagement in their health care, shared decision making with their clinicians, and better health outcomes, because patients actively engaged in their health care tend to have better health outcomes.[3]

Social media use empowers health-care consumers to engage in their care by making connections with their health-care providers and others with shared experiences and by learning more about their health.[4] Connecting patients to each other helps them share information, learn about treatments, and become more informed about diagnoses. For those living in rural or isolated areas, the Internet can be a lifeline. Finding those with similar conditions allows these patients to have the same benefits as those to whom in-person support groups are available. They can support each other living with diabetes, talk to those who have undergone similar surgeries, learn to deal with asthma, seek parenting advice, and get the emotional support needed to aid in their recovery.[5] A strong online community occurs when participants of that community are engaged and active in sharing and learning. As more members of a community connect, the sharing and support become more valuable to all.[6]

Librarians can help students in the health-care professions to develop skills in using social media to create community among themselves as students and as health-care providers and to add value to their future patients' experiences. Including social media resources in LibGuides or similar content management systems enables collections of resources to serve an information need of students in the health-care professions. Libraries could feature collections such as "Getting Started with Social Media in Health Care," "Social Media for Nurses," or "Best Social Media Sites for Your Patients" and integrate these resources into the library's website. Librarians can also teach, as part of library instruction sessions and tips for "Life after the University," how to evaluate and select appropriate social media resources. It's important to guide patients to authoritative and informative sources since the existence of poor-quality information on the Internet is widespread. Recognizing their patients' need for support and information seeking serves to improve the patient/provider relationship and aids in improved health. Additionally, students can learn ways to use social media themselves to share information and communicate in times of crisis such as disease outbreaks, creating an online community of the patients served by their clinic.[7] The medical community should not overlook social media as a tool for information seeking and community building used by patients and practitioners alike.

USE OF SOCIAL MEDIA FOR HEALTH-RELATED PURPOSES: PATIENT COMMUNITIES

In addition to patients and health-care consumers finding value in online sources, they can be empowered through the use of social media. Patients who are engaged in their own health care have better outcomes, and guiding them to effective and useful sources is an important part of patient education. Thanks to social networking sites, it's possible for online communities to form based on a shared condition or characteristic, allowing the specific user to find information relevant to them. "Interactivity also fosters active participation of users, collaboration, and the emergence of collective intelligence."[8] Librarians who serve patients and families, for example, in the public library or a hospital library that includes consumer health, can guide patients to recommended sites that they know to be trusted. They can curate social media to provide guidance for the best results. Whether a patient is looking for an active support group or just seeking to learn more about their health at the beginning of their journey, librarians can provide value in their patient education role. Patients seeking more information about their health may not immediately think of social media as a place to find it. They may be seeking pamphlets or in-person support groups. The consumer health librarian can enlighten them and let them know there are additional options for finding information and support via social media.

While popular use of Twitter, for example, includes reading about the lives of celebrities and following the news, social media's effect on the everyday lives of people who use it is increasing, including influencing their attitudes and behavior relevant to health issues. Patients use social media to find support groups, seek information on their conditions, and track progress. Forming a community and connecting with those who share experiences are also ways social media is used by health-care patients. Online support is a particularly useful tool for those in recovery and serves to connect users to others who share their circumstances. Patients who are in addiction recovery, suicide survivors, or those with chronic illnesses can find peer support through social media. Peer support is recognized as a valuable step in recovery. For patients who may be geographically isolated or in rural areas, in jobs where it's hard to get time off, or constrained by being in a small community where everyone knows each other, being able to connect online is a great resource. "Various advantages of online health communities include: linking people with similar experience together beyond the constraints of geographic proximity or social status, maintaining access to the community without concern for time, location, and schedule changes, and further enhancing health outcomes and life quality."[9] Being able to connect in online communities is one aspect of the current focus in medicine on patient-centered care. Patients obtain accurate medical information online from peers and get the support they need to aid their recovery or improved health outcome.

A newly diagnosed patient often wants to learn all they can about their condition. Health-care providers and librarians can add to their list of suggested patient resources the ability to find like-minded individuals on Twitter, either by searching text or using hashtags. The Healthcare Hashtag Project, at Symplur.com, allows searching by disease for hashtags, or searchable subject tags. Instead of just "diabetes" as an option, there are hashtags for gestational diabetes, living with diabetes, diabetes education, diabetes advocacy, Type 2 diabetes, and diabetes groups formed by location. Patient education librarians could distribute a brochure on "how to find online community" and make recommendations.

Part of a patient's experience in dealing with a new or continuing diagnosis or condition is educating family members to understand what they're going through and to learn more about their health. Through online support groups, they can share the experiences of others who have done this and benefit from those shared experiences. This online support is an additional tool to in-person support and serves to strengthen the patient's ability to offer peer support themselves, once they have explored the knowledge and experience of others.

Patients with more rare conditions may be more likely to find support online, such as those with pulmonary fibrosis. Multiple myeloma (a type of blood cancer), dermatologic conditions, and autoimmune diseases all have multiple groups dedicated to them on Facebook. Patients who never found another person with their condition can connect and no longer feel alone.[10] Facebook could be an overlooked source for this type of interaction, but librarians can guide patients and show them how to search for groups concerning their disease.

Patient involvement in online forums, which could be via Twitter, Facebook, or blogs but could also be hosted by health-care providers to connect patients, is beneficial to the provider as well as the patient.[11] Learning about new treatments, finding out how others have dealt with symptoms, and discovering ways for family members and caregivers to cope are all valuable outcomes of this online interaction.

Another beneficial experience with online support communities is for patients who "lurk" (those who read the content of online support or other types of groups but don't usually post any content themselves) or don't participate as fully as other members of the community might. These users can still gain benefit from being better informed, having an improved relationship with their health-care provider, having increased knowledge about their treatment, and feeling more in control. "In fact, online support groups play a significant role in improving patients' emotional and psychological health by providing diverse informational, instrumental, and emotional support," and one study found that those who engaged less in an online cancer support group still reaped the same benefits.[12]

Nurses, pharmacists, counselors, physician assistants, and physicians can add value to their patients' online support experiences by understanding patients' information-seeking behavior and helping to direct them to authoritative sources. Health-care professionals can also benefit from the networking functions of social media themselves by utilizing social media to keep abreast of current events in their field, to locate colleagues working on similar topics or in the same geographic area, and to find out what others are interested in. Building a strong network is key to optimizing the utilization of social media.

USE OF SOCIAL MEDIA FOR HEALTH PROFESSIONS: PRACTITIONER COMMUNITIES

Librarians with experience in the professional use of social media are in a position to educate medical practitioners about the value of networking, information sharing, and education through these channels. Training sessions at conferences or staff meetings about the importance of social media and how to use it beneficially are one way to reach this audience. Acting as a resource for social media best practices and how to maintain professionalism online is an innovative way for librarians to promote the use of technology. Continuing medical education credit may be granted for this type of instruction through a medical association or institution, which is a good way to make clinicians aware of these resources.

Clinicians can benefit from understanding their patients' information-seeking behaviors and help direct them to authoritative sources, and they can also use these tools to improve their own networking and education. "Implementing social media into the practice of medicine can only serve to benefit patients, as well as physicians."[13] Social media is also of great benefit to health-care providers and can be used to share information, to keep track of advances in one's field, to serve as a current awareness tool, to make connections with others doing similar work, and to refer patients. Networking with colleagues and others such as researchers who have shared interests enables the individual health-care provider, especially those in rural or otherwise isolated areas, to connect in ways previously unavailable to them.

Health-care providers can use social media to discuss practice issues and health-care policy, to interact with colleagues, to develop a professional network, to increase personal knowledge, to learn from experts, and to disseminate their research.[14] Twitter, for example, can be used to find people or organizations to connect with. It's possible to search geographically to find others nearby or in similar situations and to enhance the strength of one's professional network. The power of a strong professional network allows us to take advantage of the experiences and knowledge of others. Once we build a trusted network, using various tactics to ensure the reliability of the participants, we begin to acquire the benefits of their knowledge as well as our own.

Trusted Networks

To build a trusted network, providers can connect to others with similar interests doing similar work. Thanks to link-shortening services, we don't really have to say everything in 140 characters or less. Twitter can be used to send links to articles, to comment on others' content, and to connect. To optimize Twitter to its fullest extent, finding the right people to form a personal network is key. Searching by organization helps one find other like-minded users. Searching geographically can also help build a network, finding others in the same region who serve the same kind of patient population, for example. This enhances a provider's connections in their community, both virtual and physical.

A network of trusted sources can be evaluated based on the contents of their tweets, who else is part of their network, and their online participation. Once this network is established, practitioners can begin to rely on the information these sources share. A trusted source will be an advantage in the quest to keep up in a certain field and stay abreast of changes. To enhance these connections, Twitter users follow others who post about topics they're interested in. Once a valuable network participant is identified, reviewing the members of that participant's network is a good way to reach out and enlarge our own networks. It's always a work in progress, adding or deleting based on which content is most relevant.

Hashtags and Twitter

Using hashtags, or searchable subject tags, is another good way to identify more relevant content. Searching a particular topic in Twitter brings up hits that may have a certain hashtag. Searching that hashtag then results in a more refined search, with targeted results. Conference hashtags are also a good way to connect. If attendees of a conference are using Twitter, they can discover each other while they're attending the same session—based on their Twitter comments—or seek each other out in other ways to discuss common interests.

Knowing what's going on via Twitter and sharing information with colleagues and patients is a good way to take advantage of what social media has to offer. Twitter can be used for patient care and advocacy, lifelong learning, research data collection and collaboration, and scholarly recognition and impact. "These tools enable instantaneous interactions with a global community of individuals, including medical professionals, learners, and patients."[15] The use of Twitter in medical and nursing education is being explored and has the objective of improving communication between instructors and students as well as teaching students to use the tool.[16]

Another example of creating a community of patients and families is school nurses using social media to promote health and wellness.[17] Social media can be used to provide educational messages about health to the community; connect to existing social media campaigns, such as tobacco cessation or teen pregnancy; and inform about disease outbreaks. These uses strengthen the community and enhance the professional standing of the school nursing profession, improving the flow of health information in a community.

Recommended Tools for Practitioners

Twitter is perhaps the most popular social media tool, and its use has expanded beyond individuals to conferences and organizations and even as a publishing platform. As previously discussed, hashtags are a way to index tweets by subject and make it easier for like-minded individuals to connect via Twitter. Finding a hashtag can be done in a variety of ways. Just searching a subject or topic is one way, and you can then check the results to see what hashtag frequent posters are using.

The Symplur Healthcare Hashtag Project is also a way to find out what hashtags are currently in use. Symplur.com is a project aimed at facilitating communication between health-care providers and patients and enhancing and improving providers' participation in social media in order to educate themselves and to steer the public toward better resources. The Healthcare Hashtag Project allows registration of a hashtag with a description of its intent. It's a free platform for patients, families, caregivers, health-care providers, and other members of the medical community. Hashtags are divided into categories for general, diseases, conferences, and Twitter chats.

A popular Twitter hashtag for medical librarians is #medlibs, for all who are interested in big data, data management, health information, health librarianship, health literacy, or medical libraries. Librarians new to the medical field, or those who would like to expand their knowledge on this topic, can connect with their colleagues using this hashtag.

Conference hashtags are very useful, both for attendees and those not able to attend. All of the tweets regarding the conference are easily searchable during or after the conference, as long as attendees use the hashtag in their tweets. The conference organizers can choose and submit their own hashtag via the Symplur website, publicize the tag to attendees and others, and start sharing. Statistics and transcripts are provided for evaluation and reference purposes. Conference hashtags are searchable by conference name and date.

And finally, another way to participate more fully in what Twitter has to offer is to take part in Twitter chats, where all the participants use the same hashtag at a specified time. Health-related chats are listed on the Symplur website under the Healthcare Hashtag Project,[18] which also provides transcripts of the chats. Chats usually last an hour and are advertised on Twitter and in blogs, and participants can join the conversation but also just see what others are doing. Past chats can be searched as well.

Twitter chats are a good way to expand a Twitter network and also connect with those outside the librarian field, for example, by joining patient or health-care provider chats. There is usually a chance to make a comment or point to a resource, and those attending the chat see a librarian in action.

BARRIERS AND PRIVACY CONCERNS

Many medical providers have well-founded concerns about online security and about patient and provider confidentiality, as well as concerns about avoiding scrutiny or professional jeopardy due to social media use. By using common sense and conservative social media practices, Twitter and Facebook can be a safe environment to share and to learn. The Federation of State Medical Boards has an informative document about the use of social media by physicians and other medical/health professionals.[19] By utilizing the available guidelines and suggested practices, medical providers can behave ethically and with a sensitivity to privacy on social media. Health professions students learn how to keep confidentiality in their training. Librarians can help make instructors and students aware of the options and how to use social media as a tool while still ensuring patient privacy is not violated.

Following the provisions of the Health Insurance Portability and Accountability Act (HIPAA) and protecting patient privacy is something most health-care providers do on a daily basis. As an important part of their educations, residents, medical students, and other health-care professional students are taught to practice professionalism and observe strict standards of patient confidentiality. The example of an elevator is often given in discussions of ethical behavior because of the public nature of such a prevalent feature of hospitals. While most experienced providers are clear on the rules of HIPAA in the workplace, they may not be as familiar with what constitutes privacy in social media, which they may also be using to network professionally. A general rule of thumb to follow is if you wouldn't say it in a crowded elevator, don't say it on Facebook or Twitter.[20] No identifiable information should be disclosed without the permission of the patient. Even if they are not identified by name, unless details of the patient visit or condition are changed, they could still be identified. While there is great benefit to the sharing and educational aspects of social media, health-care students and professionals still need to observe professionalism while using social media. Examples of unacceptable use include using social media to contact a patient for personal reasons, complaining about a patient online, using social media to post pictures of the health-care provider "partying" or appearing drunk, giving medical advice to someone who is not a patient, and inadvertently identifying a patient when the purpose is education (e.g., filming a procedure for students when the patient's face is visible). Using good judgment will help avoid situations like these and allow social media to be used as a valuable tool.

Sharing diagnostic images and disseminating research findings are both functions that many health-care providers accomplish via social media. According to Crane and Gardner, pathologists are a group whose use of social media to share images is increasing rapidly.[21] This issue has been debated within the profession, yet the power of social media for sharing images and research and educating the public is beneficial and some would say outweighs the possible harm. Several suggestions are made by Crane and Gardner to avoid the potential for privacy violations: never use the date of the actual visit, delay posting about highly unusual cases that may be reported in the news, avoid facial images or unique tattoos, avoid precise ages, don't mention geographical locations, and modify clinical history to further disguise the patient. This way, the educational benefit can still be realized without privacy being violated.

Librarians who serve health professions students and health-care professionals are in a key position to educate and inform about how to best utilize the benefits of social media in health care. Underutilization of the medium means not taking advantage of a powerful tool for information exchange, but fears remain. "Despite social media's increasingly prominent role in medicine, barriers exist that limit wider adoption of use by medical professionals."[22] Additional barriers exist to the use of social media: unfamiliarity with the concept, lack of technical skill, disbelief that using social media won't result in more information overload. Phases of the adoption of social media include learning the platform exists, observing how others use it, using it to broadcast information, and finally moving to the phase of sharing and engaging in the social network community, focusing on relationships and collaboration. Finally, while some may see participating in online health communities as creating a barrier between patient and provider, most evidence shows that seeking additional information in fact improves the relationship.[23] Remaining informed of the possibilities of social media and becoming experienced users themselves enables librarians to promote this avenue of increased information and communication, resulting in better communication with patients, which leads to improved patient care.

ROLE OF LIBRARIANS

Through advocating, identifying, and partnering with social media champions within their user groups, librarians can provide tools to determine value in online sources. They can connect with students and faculty within their institutions via social media and demonstrate its utility in sharing important information. Through instructional methods such as LibGuides or other content management systems, librarians can highlight social media as a resource for health professions students. They can stress the role of social media in information exchange and professional networking in instructional sessions. They can teach about the importance of social media in building patient communities to provider peer support and patient education and show them how to find these communities.

Teaching about the tools and skills to use social media to its full advantage is a perfect role for librarians. They can advocate for the inclusion of these skills in the curriculum, teaching students to use social media professionally to enhance their own networking and education for their patients and also how to avoid pitfalls and address privacy concerns by being aware of patient privacy regulations and knowing how to protect confidentiality.

Stakeholders in today's health-care environment—including clinicians, educators, and administrators—may not be fully aware of the importance of social media. But the use continues to grow, and knowledge of this phenomenon is necessary to understand its place in health care, consumer awareness, and even health-care costs.

Librarians' role is to educate the students, instructors, and clinicians they serve to be fully informed of the ethical, educational, peer support, and professional development aspects of social media in health care.

CONCLUSION

We've shown how social media can empower patients, making them more likely to be engaged in their health, ask questions, learn about new treatments and participate in their care, which in turn results in better health outcomes and lower health-care costs. The role of social media in recovery has been recognized for its importance and provides support and healing for patients and families who might not otherwise have access to peer support. Patients in rural areas or who are otherwise isolated are particularly at risk for losing the benefit of peer support if not for online communities.

Health-care providers as well stand to benefit greatly from the increased use and presence of social media in their profession, as well as being able to refer patients to authoritative and useful support groups. Fear of privacy concerns and lack of expertise should not stop providers from utilizing this powerful tool. The use of social media by health-care professionals holds great potential for enhancing the knowledge of providers and subsequently enhancing the care provided to patients.

NOTES

1. "Health Fact Sheet," Pew Research Center, accessed October 21, 2016, www.pewinternet.org/fact-sheets/health-fact-sheet/.

2. "The Social Life of Health Information," Pew Research Center, accessed October 21, 2016, www.pewresearch.org/fact-tank/2014/01/15/the-social-life-of-health-information/.

3. "Patient Engagement," *Health Policy Briefs*, Health Affairs, accessed October 21, 2016, www.healthaffairs.org/healthpolicybriefs/brief.php?brief_id=86.

4. Judith H. Hibbard and Jessica Greene, "What the Evidence Shows about Patient Activation: Better Health Outcomes and Care Experiences; Fewer Data on Costs," *Health Affairs (Millwood)* 32, no. 2 (2013): 207–14.

5. Jae Eun Chung, "Social Networking in Online Support Groups for Health: How Online Social Networking Benefits Patients," *Journal of Health Communication* 19, no. 6 (2014): 639–59.

6. Christopher E. Beaudoin and Chen-Chao Tao, "Benefiting from Social Capital in Online Support Groups: An Empirical Study of Cancer Patients," *CyberPsychology & Behavior* 10, no. 4 (2007): 587–90; Grietje Bouma, Lein M. Admiraal, Elisabeth G. deVries, Carolien P. Schroder, Annemiek M. E. Walenkamp, and Anna K. Reyners, "Internet-Based Support Programs to Alleviate Psychosocial and Physical Symptoms in Cancer Patients: A Literature Analysis," *Critical Reviews in Oncology/Hematology* 95, no. 1 (2015): 26–37.

7. "Top 5 Ways Social Media Is Used by Healthcare Professionals," University of Scranton Online Resources Center, accessed October 21, 2016, elearning.scranton.edu/resource/business-leadership/top-5-ways-social-media-is-used-by-healthcare-professionals.

8. Bernard Lo and Lindsay Parham, "The Impact of Web 2.0 on the Doctor-Patient Relationship," *Journal of Law, Medicine & Ethics* 38, no. 1 (2010): 17–26.

9. Jing Zhao, Sejin Ha, and Richard Widdows, "Building Trusting Relationships in Online Health Communities," *Cyberpsychology, Behavior, and Social Networking* 16, no. 9 (2013): 650–57.

10. Shaohai Jiang, "The Role of Social Media Use in Improving Cancer Survivors' Emotional Well-Being: A Moderated Mediation Study," *Journal of Cancer Survivorship* [Epub ahead of print] (2017); Chung, "Social Networking," 642.

11. Karen Albright, Tarik Walker, Susan Baird, Linda Eres, Tara Farnsworth, Kaitlin Fier, Dolly Kervitsky, Marjorie Korn, David J. Lederer, Mark McCormick, John F. Steiner, Thomas Vierzba, Frederick S. Wamboldt, and Jeffrey J. Swigris, "Seeking and Sharing: Why the Pulmonary Fibrosis Community Engages the Web 2.0 Environment," *BMC Pulmonary Medicine* 16, no. 4 (2016).

12. Jeong Yeob Han, Jiran Hou, Eunkyung Kim, and David H. Gustafson, "Lurking as an Active Participation Process: A Longitudinal Investigation of Engagement with an Online Cancer Support Group," *Health Communication* 29, no. 9 (2014): 911–23.

13. Kevin R. Steehler, Matthew K. Steehler, Matthew L. Pierce, and Earl H. Harley, "Social Media's Role in Otolaryngology-Head and Neck Surgery: Informing Clinicians, Empowering Patients," *Otolaryngology Head and Neck Surgery* 149, no. 4 (2013): 521–24.

14. C. Lee Ventola, "Social Media and Health Care Professionals: Benefits, Risks, and Best Practices," *Pharmacy and Therapeutics* 39, no. 7 (2014): 491–520.

15. Matthew E. Peters, Elisabeth Uible, and Margaret S. Chisolm, "A Twitter Education: Why Psychiatrists Should Tweet," *Current Psychiatry Reports* 17, no. 12 (2015): 94.

16. Julee Waldrop and Diane Wink, "Twitter: An Application to Encourage Information Seeking among Nursing Students," *Nurse Educator* 41, no. 3 (2016): 160–63.

17. Regina Wysocki, "Social Media for School Nurses: Promoting School Health in the 21st Century," *NASN School Nurse* 30, no. 3 (2015): 180–88.

18. "Symplur Healthcare Hashtag Project," accessed October 21, 2016, www.symplur.com/healthcare-hashtags/.

19. "Model Policy Guidelines for the Appropriate Use of Social Media and Social Networking in Medical Practice," Federation of State Medical Boards, accessed October 21, 2016, www.fsmb.org/Media/Default/PDF/Publications/pub-social-media-guidelines.pdf.

20. "3 Core Legal Issues for Hospital Marketing Programs," Becker's Hospital Review, February 10, 2012, accessed February 9, 2017, www.beckershospitalreview.com/hospital-management-administration/3-core-legal-issues-for-hospital-marketing-programs.html.

21. Genevieve M. Crane and Jerad M. Gardner, "Pathology Image-Sharing on Social Media: Recommendations for Protecting Privacy while Motivating Education," *AMA Journal of Ethics* 18, no. 8 (2016): 817–25.

22. Matthew E. Peters, Elisabeth Uible, and Margaret S. Chisolm, "A Twitter Education: Why Psychiatrists Should Tweet," *Current Psychiatry Reports* 17, no. 12 (2015): 94.

23. Douglas J. Rupert, Rebecca R. Moultrie, Jennifer Gard Read, Jacqueline B. Amoozegar, Alexandra S. Bornkessel, Amie C. O'Donoghue, and Helen W. Sullivan, "Perceived Healthcare Provider Reactions to Patient and Caregiver Use of Online Health Communities," *Patient Education & Counseling* 96, no. 3 (2014): 320–26.

BIBLIOGRAPHY

Albright, Karen, Tarik Walker, Susan Baird, Linda Eres, Tara Farnsworth, Kaitlin Fier, Dolly Kervitsky, Marjorie Korn, David J. Lederer, Mark McCormick, John F. Steiner, Thomas Vierzba, Frederick S. Wamboldt, and Jeffrey J. Swigris. "Seeking and Sharing: Why the Pulmonary Fibrosis Community Engages the Web 2.0 Environment." *BMC Pulmonary Medicine* 16, no. 4 (2016).

Beaudoin, Christopher E., and Chen-Chao Tao. "Benefiting from Social Capital in Online Support Groups: An Empirical Study of Cancer Patients." *CyberPsychology & Behavior* 10, no. 4 (2007): 587–90.

Bouma, Grietje, Lein M. Admiraal, Elisabeth G. deVries, Carolien P. Schroder, Annemiek M. E. Walenkamp, and Anna K. Reyners. "Internet-Based Support Programs to Alleviate Psychosocial and Physical Symptoms in Cancer Patients: A Literature Analysis." *Critical Reviews in Oncology/Hematology* 95, no. 1 (2015): 26–37.

Chung, Jae Eun. "Social Networking in Online Support Groups for Health: How Online Social Networking Benefits Patients." *Journal of Health Communication* 19, no. 6 (2014): 639–59.

Crane, Genevieve M., and Jerad M. Gardner. "Pathology Image-Sharing on Social Media: Recommendations for Protecting Privacy while Motivating Education." *AMA Journal of Ethics* 18, no. 8 (2016): 817–25.

Han, Jeong Yeob, Jiran Hou, Eunkyung Kim, and David H. Gustafson. "Lurking as an Active Participation Process: A Longitudinal Investigation of Engagement with an Online Cancer Support Group." *Health Communication* 29, no. 9 (2014): 911–23.

"Health Fact Sheet." Pew Research Center. Accessed October 21, 2016. www.pewinternet.org/fact-sheets/health-fact-sheet/.

Hibbard, Judith H., and Jessica Greene. "What the Evidence Shows about Patient Activation: Better Health Outcomes and Care Experiences; Fewer Data on Costs." *Health Affairs (Millwood)* 32, no. 2 (2013): 207–14.

Jiang, Shaohai. "The Role of Social Media Use in Improving Cancer Survivors' Emotional Well-Being: A Moderated Mediation Study." *Journal of Cancer Survivorship* [Epub ahead of print] (2017).

Lo, Bernard, and Lindsay Parham. "The Impact of Web 2.0 on the Doctor-Patient Relationship." *Journal of Law, Medicine & Ethics* 38, no. 1 (2010): 17–26.

"Model Policy Guidelines for the Appropriate Use of Social Media and Social Networking in Medical Practice." Federation of State Medical Boards. Accessed October 21, 2016. www .fsmb.org/Media/Default/PDF/Publications/pub-social-media-guidelines.pdf.

"Patient Engagement." *Health Policy Briefs*. Health Affairs. Accessed October 21, 2016. www .healthaffairs.org/healthpolicybriefs/brief.php?brief_id=86

Peters, Matthew E., Elisabeth Uible, and Margaret S. Chisolm. "A Twitter Education: Why Psychiatrists Should Tweet." *Current Psychiatry Reports* 17, no. 12 (2015): 94.

Rupert, Douglas J., Rebecca R. Moultrie, Jennifer Gard Read, Jacqueline B. Amoozegar, Alexandra S. Bornkessel, Amie C. O'Donoghue, and Helen W. Sullivan. "Perceived Healthcare Provider Reactions to Patient and Caregiver Use of Online Health Communities." *Patient Education & Counseling* 96, no. 3 (2014): 320–26.

"The Social Life of Health Information." Pew Research Center. Accessed October 21, 2016. www.pewresearch.org/fact-tank/2014/01/15/the-social-life-of-health-information/.

Steehler, Kevin R., Matthew K. Steehler, Matthew L. Pierce, and Earl H. Harley. "Social Media's Role in Otolaryngology-Head and Neck Surgery: Informing Clinicians, Empowering Patients." *Otolaryngology Head and Neck Surgery* 149, no. 4 (2013): 521–24.

"Symplur Healthcare Hashtag Project." Accessed October 21, 2016. www.symplur.com/ healthcare-hashtags/.

"3 Core Legal Issues for Hospital Marketing Programs." Becker's Hospital Review. February 10, 2012, accessed February 9, 2017. www.beckershospitalreview.com/hospital-manage ment-administration/3-core-legal-issues-for-hospital-marketing-programs.html.

"Top 5 Ways Social Media is Used by Healthcare Professionals." University of Scranton Online Resources Center. Accessed October 21, 2016. elearning.scranton.edu/resource/ business-leadership/top-5-ways-social-media-is-used-by-healthcare-professionals.

Ventola, C. Lee. "Social Media and Health Care Professionals: Benefits, Risks, and Best Practices." *Pharmacy and Therapeutics* 39, no. 7 (2014): 491–520.

Waldrop, Julee, and Diane Wink. "Twitter: An Application to Encourage Information Seeking Among Nursing Students." *Nurse Educator* 41, no. 3 (2016): 160–63.

Wysocki, Regina. "Social Media for School Nurses: Promoting School Health in the 21st Century." *NASN School Nurse* 30, no. 3 (2015): 180–88.

Zhao, Jing, Sejin Ha, and Richard Widdows. "Building Trusting Relationships in Online Health Communities." *Cyberpsychology, Behavior, and Social Networking* 16, no. 9 (2013): 650–57.

5

Adding Value with Advertising

Using Paid Promotions to Build Your Online Community

Christopher Chan and Joanna Hare

OVERVIEW

Paid advertising is an unfamiliar concept to many librarians, especially to those working in schools, colleges, and universities. Traditional advertising on television, radio, newspapers, and so forth generally only makes sense for libraries serving a large population, such as public library systems. Early forms of online advertising were similarly unsuited to smaller libraries because of the large and loosely defined audiences. Social media advertising is a very different proposition, as these platforms allow advertisers to specify with precision the audience they want to reach, in some cases to the institutional level.

Although social network services (SNS) make paid advertising a possibility for libraries that do not usually engage in the practice, you may still question whether it is worth the money and effort. It is certainly true that libraries can get a lot of value out of social media without paying, but unpaid social media strategies may only be able to take you so far. Social media advertising can also be surprisingly cost-effective even with a relatively small budget, and you will receive concrete feedback on how your advertising campaign performs. Some may be uncomfortable with spending even a modest amount of money on something as ephemeral and intangible as online adverts. However, your library is probably already spending similar amounts printing posters and ordering souvenirs—how is spending on social media advertising any different?

Moreover, there is tremendous potential for SNS advertising to turbocharge user engagement with your library's social media efforts. For online community building to be effective, your followers need to see and interact with your posts. While paid advertising can never substitute for compelling content, it is a tool that libraries should consider deploying to ensure their social media efforts receive the attention from their community that they deserve.

Most of the social media platforms libraries are likely to engage with offer paid advertising, but our focus in this chapter will be on Facebook. This is mainly due to our experience being exclusively with Facebook advertising and also because Facebook is the dominant social media platform. There are currently no signs that it will relinquish the top spot anytime soon—at the end of 2016 it boasted more than 1.1 billion daily active users globally.[1] We have also found Facebook's advertising toolkit to be robust and user friendly. Most importantly, Facebook allows for highly specific targeting based on the data users have provided about themselves. The options available in this regard are more plentiful than even competing social networks such as Twitter, partly because there is an expectation on Facebook that users present their real identity. This is vital for libraries that cannot afford to waste limited funding on ads that fail to reach their specific community members with a high degree of accuracy.

In what follows, we will share our experiences with advertising on Facebook at our institutions, Hong Kong Baptist University (HKBU) and City University of Hong Kong (CityU). We begin with a beginner's guide to creating and managing adverts on Facebook, including tips for maximizing the effectiveness of your advertising campaigns. We then present the quantitative results of recent adverts run at both institutions, contrasting the experience of a library with years of SNS advertising experience with a library running its very first campaign. Finally, we consider whether students feel that it is appropriate for libraries to be advertising in this way and present evidence from a survey conducted at the authors' institutions.

Both authors are at academic libraries, but we believe that the techniques and observations described here will be broadly applicable to different library types.

FACEBOOK ADVERTISING: A BEGINNER'S GUIDE

As discussed by Young and Rossmann,[2] the existing body of research about library Facebook usage suggests that many libraries are using Facebook as an announcement portal and are yet to explore the full benefits of Facebook's capacity for community building. With this in mind, paid Facebook advertising provides an opportunity to engage audiences with content that goes beyond messages about opening hours and new acquisitions. Facebook advertising also provides greater reassurance that your messages are reaching your existing audience, as well as people who aren't already fans of your page and—perhaps more valuably—aren't active users of your library.

A step-by-step account of using Facebook's advertising platform will quickly become obsolete as the interface is frequently updated and new features are being introduced all the time. Instead, we will focus on the core concepts that will remain constant: **goals**, **audience**, and **budget and schedule**. The screenshots used to illustrate this section were current as of December 2016.

Pro Tip! You can explore the entire Facebook advertising platform without having to commit to paying for advertising. The simplest way to begin is to access the "Create Ad" option under the small arrow menu on your Facebook page (as shown in figure 5.1)

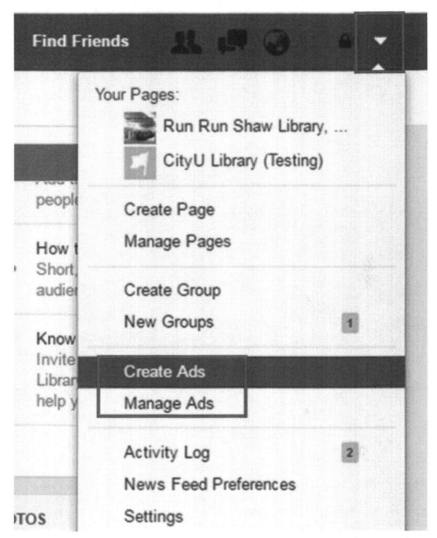

Figure 5.1.   How to access the "Create Ads" interface (as of December 2016)

Part One: Define Your Goals

The goals that you set will determine the **type of advertisement** you choose in Facebook's Ads Manager (see figure 5.2). The ability to publicly "Like" something is the defining feature of Facebook, and the number of Likes that your page has received is a straightforward measure to help judge how well you are doing.[3] To increase your page likes, you can choose the **"Promote your Page"** advertisement. This tends to be a more costly approach, but once connected to your page, your "fans"

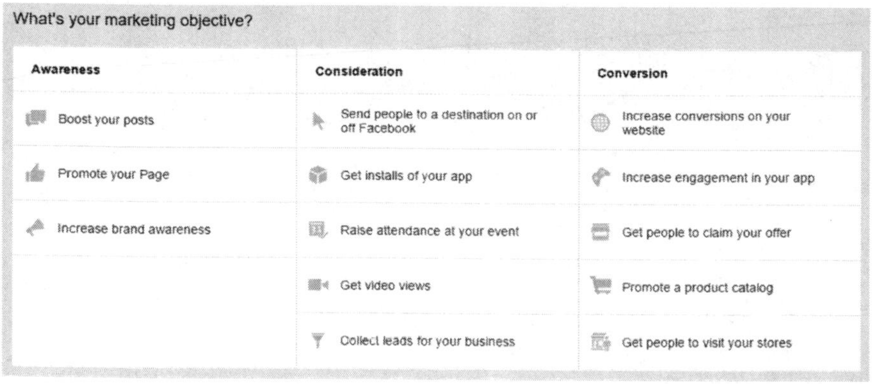

What's your marketing objective?		
Awareness	**Consideration**	**Conversion**
Boost your posts	Send people to a destination on or off Facebook	Increase conversions on your website
Promote your Page	Get installs of your app	Increase engagement in your app
Increase brand awareness	Raise attendance at your event	Get people to claim your offer
	Get video views	Promote a product catalog
	Collect leads for your business	Get people to visit your stores

Figure 5.2. "What's your marketing objective?": Facebook's options for creating paid advertisements. Facebook has many options for creating advertisements, such as driving traffic to a website or getting installs of an app. These may be worth considering depending on your goals.

are much more likely to see your Facebook content organically (i.e., naturally in the course of interacting with the social network). Furthermore, based on the News Feed algorithm, their connection with your page and any subsequent interactions with your content may be made visible to their Facebook friends.[4] Their friends may also be people that you want to attract as part of your community-building efforts.

To ensure your messages about specific events or services are reaching your community, you can choose to promote one of your regular posts through what Facebook calls "**Boosted Posts**." This allows you to promote a single post on your page to help it reach both your existing fans and people who have not "'Liked" your page. This tends to be a very cost-effective option and is a much smaller monetary commitment. Concrete examples of both approaches are provided in the discussion of our recent adverts.

Part Two: Define Your Audience

Facebook's advert targeting provides the greatest potential for building community, allowing you to tap into specific demographics to whom to deliver tailored content. For university libraries, targeting an audience is relatively straightforward (you can simply specify that Facebook show your advertisement to people who have self-identified as students at your institution). Libraries with a target audience defined by geographic region rather than institutional affiliation might explore some of the more detailed demographic information, creating complex audiences based on the messages they wish to share. The basic audience targeting options are geographic location, age, gender, and language. Beyond this, users can be targeted based on profession, political affiliation, interests (e.g., "reading" or "science fiction movies"), even whether they have experienced a particular "life event" recently such as getting married or moving away from home. Building on this, targeting facets can be combined to create a very narrow audience, such as "parents of teens who live within twenty kilometers of your library." See figure 5.3 for the interface used for choosing targeting options.

There are of course some limitations. Targeting students at a particular institution relies on students providing that information to Facebook, and users may opt not to share such information. Additionally, targeting students aged seventeen to twenty-two may neglect mature-age students, but a broader bracket such as seventeen to thirty may include alumni, who may not be eligible for the same level of service that is promoted to current students. However, as discussed in the introduction to this chapter, the fact that Facebook supports at least *some* level of targeted advertising is a feature that other "traditional" advertising methods lack.

Understandably, the use of personal data in this way may leave many library and information professionals feeling uncomfortable. To try and address this, we conducted two focus groups and a survey to explore student attitudes toward targeted Facebook advertising. We found that while a majority of students expressed some level of discomfort with the use of targeted advertising *in general*, they were much more comfortable with the *library* promoting messages on Facebook. A more fulsome discussion of these results is shared in the last section of this chapter.

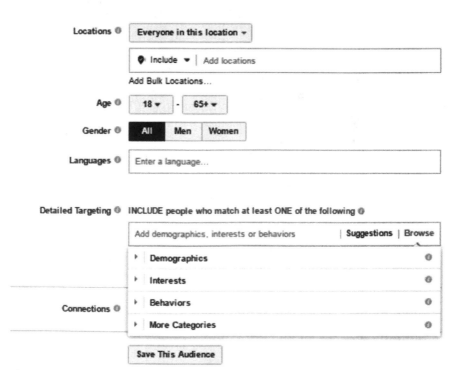

Figure 5.3. Define your audience: Options to target your Facebook advertising

Part Three: Define Your Budget and Schedule

The timing of your advertisements must also be considered in order to maximize their community-building potential. As found in research by Young et al.[5] and Chan,[6] Facebook advertising is subject to diminishing returns. In Facebook advertising carried out between 2011 and 2016 at HKBU Library, it was found that the optimal time frame for a Page Promotion is two to four weeks, while a Boosted Post performs best over one to seven days. Furthermore, just as with more traditional forms of library marketing, it makes sense for online advertisements to coincide with certain times of the year that your library is already more "visible," such as during orientation week.

In terms of budgeting for your advertisement, you have two options: a "daily" budget or a "lifetime" budget. A daily budget means you specify how much you want to spend each day, and once you reach that amount, your ad will stop being shown for that day. A lifetime budget means your ad will continue being shown in your specified time frame until your maximum amount is reached. You will notice that as you change the budget, the "Potential Reach" also changes: a higher budget means a greater Potential Reach. Facebook has a number of Advanced Options you can use to specify how your ad is delivered (placement, time of day, etc.). However, for beginners it is recommended you use Facebook's default settings—in general they will optimize your ad based on their own algorithms. See figure 5.4 for an example of the "Budget & Schedule" interface.

The monetary budget for Facebook advertising will of course vary at each individual institution, but understanding this basic structure of pricing will help you get an idea of how much you want to spend.[7]

Some Practical Considerations for Your First Campaign

- Facebook's Ad Manager is tied to a personal Facebook profile—not a Facebook page. You can delegate others to allow them access, either as an Advertiser (who can create and edit adverts) or as an Analyst (who can only view statistics about advert performance).[8] These options are useful if a team of colleagues is involved in managing your Facebook page.

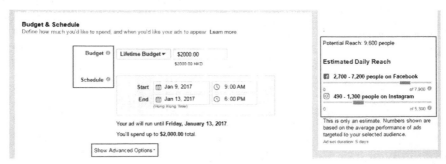

Figure 5.4.   Defining your budget and schedule. Amounts shown are in Hong Kong dollars.

- Facebook has a "billing threshold," which means you are billed when your ad spending reaches certain amounts. This means you may be billed in several smaller transactions rather than a single transaction. Payment methods, billing thresholds, and payment timing vary from country to country.[9]

Advertising Results: Choose Your Metric

The Ads Manager will provide a huge amount of data both during and after your campaign that are useful for evaluating how your efforts were received by your community. The metric for a Page Promotion is simple: the number of page Likes your campaign attracted. Measuring the success of a Boosted Post is less straightforward, as there are three relevant metrics:

- **Likes, Reactions, or Engagements:** the number of people who "Liked" your page, "reacted" to your post (i.e., "Liked," "Loved," "Sad," "Angry"), or clicked a link in your post.
- **Total Reach:** the number of people your advertisement was delivered to (typically much higher than Likes and Reactions).
- **Cost per Like/Reaction/Engagement:** Your total spend divided by the number of Likes, Reactions, or engagements.

Although the "Like" is sometimes viewed as the ultimate Facebook metric, the "Total Reach" or "Link Clicks" oftentimes gives a more realistic idea of the value of the campaign. People can be interested in your message without explicitly "reacting" to it. Facebook itself emphasizes the overall cost per Like/Reaction/Engagement, which breaks down how many times Facebook users interacted with sponsored content. However, some engagements can be considered more valuable than others. Link clicks, for example, might be more desirable than Reactions as they show that the user has been interested enough in the content to go and check it out for themselves. Ultimately, the most appropriate measure to use will be determined by the purpose for which the advert was placed—real-world examples will be given in the next section.

Depending on your goals and how you defined your audience, you might also explore how particular groups reacted to your advertisement. For example, you could see which age brackets or people from which region were engaging most with your content.

Pro Tip! Facebook's free "Adverts" app has a much more user-friendly interface for exploring your advertising results (see figure 5.5).

Facebook Advertising for Community Building: Some Ideas

Just as librarians get creative with the content they share on Facebook, a Facebook advertising strategy can also be creative—again, they don't all have to be "broadcast" messages. A Facebook advertising strategy can serve as a complementary component of a library's broader strategy for building community using social media. (See chapter 2 for a full discussion of building a social media strategy.) As observed by Young

Figure 5.5. It can be easier to find useful information on the performance of your adverts via Facebook's Adverts app. Amounts shown are in Hong Kong dollars.

et al.,[10] posts about library events and library staff often have high engagement. Identifying what content is engaging to the users you are already reaching is a great way to identify the type of content that will be meaningful to the broader community. Libraries wanting to experiment with Facebook advertising for community building might also explore some of the following suggestions:

- Promote community-building events within your library and your community, such as student support programs at examination period or "food for fines" campaigns.
- Share "behind-the-scenes at the library" content, such as pictures from a party recognizing a longstanding staff member or some images of hidden gems in your storage collection.
- Include user-generated content, such as asking your community to share their book recommendations for the year or run a competition for people to submit creative entries.
- Share content from or features on "influencers" or well-known people within your campus or library community.

In the following sections, we share the results of Facebook advertising campaigns undertaken at our institutions during 2016 that show Facebook advertising can be very effective in sharing library messages with broad but targeted community audiences.

FACEBOOK ADVERT EXAMPLES

To illustrate some of the concepts and ideas discussed above, in this section we examine in detail some recent adverts conducted at our institutions, both of which are in Hong Kong. HKBU Library has used paid Facebook advertising since 2011. In contrast, CityU Library ran its very first campaign in October 2016. This provided an opportunity to compare the performance of adverts from an institution with relatively greater advertising experience to a first-timer.

Page Promotion

As described in the preceding section, promoting your page can be selected as a goal for your Facebook advert. You can then designate a short piece of text and a selection of images for the promotional piece. These will be displayed in various places—in your target audience's news feed (both desktop and mobile) and in the space for adverts in the right-hand column of the desktop version. Adverts Manager will provide data for each image separately—experiment with different ones to see what gets the best result. Figure 5.6 presents examples of the page post adverts produced by HKBU Library and CityU Library for this campaign.

Hong Kong Baptist University Library (HKBU Library)
Sponsored

浸會大學圖書館: 提供多元化服務推動學習與研究 — HKBU Library:
Promoting Learning, Enabling Research

Hong Kong Baptist University Library (HKBU Library)
Library
6,438 people like this.   👍 Like Page

 Run Run Shaw Library, City University of Hong Kong
Sponsored

香港城市大學邵逸夫圖書館

Run Run Shaw Library, City University of Hong Kong
Library
2,309 people like this.   👍 Like Page

Figure 5.6.   Examples of Page Promotion adverts. We chose images that were easily recognized as being our libraries.

We were interested in comparing the results of our respective institutions, and so we decided to make our campaigns as similar as possible. Although it was not possible to run the campaigns at exactly the same time, other elements such as the target audience (undergraduate students), campaign length, total budget, number of advert creatives, and so on were identical. Refer to table 5.1 for the results.

The difference in performance between the two universities is immediately obvious. The cost per Like achieved by HKBU Library in its most recent campaign is much higher than in some of its earlier campaigns, where the cost per Like fell to as little as HK$1.91.[11] It is possible that having conducted several such campaigns over the years the pool of potentially interested students at HKBU Library is smaller. CityU Library's better performance might be explained by the fact that this is the first time its audience has been targeted.

CityU Library was pleased with the results of their first campaign and is committed to run similar Page Promotion campaigns at the beginning of the two 2017 semesters. HKBU Library is somewhat concerned about the high cost per Like compared to its previous campaigns. While it is still not too high, the cost per Like will be closely monitored to ensure that value for money is maintained. It is possible that after running adverts for several years, a saturation point may have been reached.

Boosted Posts

A boosted post will appear in the news feed of your targeted audience in the same way as stories that appear organically. The only difference will be that the word "Sponsored" will be displayed near the top of the post (see figure 5.7 below). One interesting point to note is that this type of advertisement is eligible to appear on Instagram, the photo-sharing app acquired by Facebook in 2012, giving your post additional exposure.[12]

As explained in the previous section, the context in which the advert was placed will determine which metrics you focus on when evaluating the success of your promoted posts. For those advertising events such as seminars and workshops, clicks through to the registration link will be more important than reactions. Conversely, for posts raising awareness of certain initiatives (such as the HKBU Library adverts for its blog and bookface competition) reach and reactions are of greater use in measuring success.

Table 5.1. The Results of Two Page Promotion Adverts at HKBU and CityU Libraries

Institution	Campaign Dates	Total Spent	Total Page Likes	Cost Per Like
HKBU	August 31–September 18, 2016	HK$2,000	230	HK$8.70
CityU	October 17–November 7, 2016	HK$2,000	415	HK$4.82

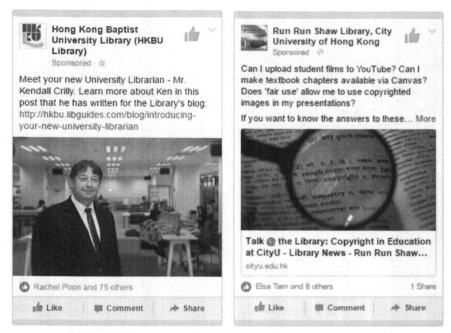

Figure 5.7.   Examples of post boosting. To your audience these look identical to any other post in their news feed, apart from the word "Sponsored" under the page title.

For CityU Library, Boosted Posts have been very valuable, due to the high reach. However, the click-through rate has not been as high as they would like. Therefore, they will try to ensure future Boosted Posts are crafted in such a way to encourage link clicks and sharing. In the advertisement in figure 5.7 (above), CityU Library experimented with targeting staff members to see if such an approach would be suitable for promoting a one-off event. The reach was much smaller due to the smaller audience size, but the click-through rate was relatively high. Depending on future needs, CityU Library may adopt this approach again but will mainly focus on targeting students.

HKBU Library has been selectively boosting posts for a number of years and will continue to do so. As the numbers from the latest boosts show, it is possible to generate significant awareness and engagement at a relatively low cost. A great deal of effort goes into community engagement efforts like the blog and the bookface competition (which was a freshman orientation activity), and boosting these through social media channels helps to ensure that they get a commensurate level of attention.

Although all of the statistics described above provide direct and tangible evidence of engagement, they cannot provide answers to some important questions. Does our community find Facebook advertising intrusive, or have they come to accept adverts as a matter of course for social networks? Or perhaps they accept advertising by businesses and corporations but find it odd when their university's library promotes in

Table 5.2. The Results for a Selection of Posts That Were Promoted at Our Institutions in the Fall of 2016

| Campaign | Target Audience | Reach | | Engagements | | | Cost per Engagement |
		Organic	Paid	Reactions	Link Clicks	Page Likes	
CityU: Mendeley/Refworks Workshop, November 2–4, 2016	All CityU students and staff	310	**1,877**	52	6	2	HK$1.5
CityU: Copyright Seminar, November 4–7, 2016	CityU staff	148	**945**	8	13	7	HK$4.76
HKBU: New UL blog post, November 18–20, 2016	All HKBU students and staff	1,516	**5,088**	82	42	4	HK$2.09
HKBU: Bookface competition, September 2–4, 2016	HKBU undergraduates	243	**4,451**	29	50	0	HK$2.74

this way. We also felt it important to address the privacy and personal information concerns alluded to earlier in the chapter. To this end, we conducted a small qualitative study of our students, making use of focus groups and an online survey.

STUDENT ATTITUDES TOWARD
LIBRARY USE OF FACEBOOK ADVERTISING

Understanding the reservations that information professionals might rightly have regarding the use of personal information to target students with adverts, we sought to ask our students directly what they thought. First, each institution organized a single focus group with a small number of students (CityU Library: four students; HKBU Library: six students). Each group worked through semistructured questions that the authors had agreed upon beforehand. Our findings informed the development of an online survey. This was open to all undergraduates at both institutions, and it was promoted to this user group with targeted Facebook advertising. A total of 1,131 valid responses were received.[13]

Highlights of Survey Results

A complete analysis of the results of the survey are beyond the scope of this chapter; however, the following observations are of particular relevance to libraries considering using Facebook advertising.

Most respondents indicated that their usage of Facebook had either stayed the same (56 percent) or increased (29 percent) in the past twelve months. Only 15 percent said their use of Facebook had declined. This alleviates concerns that Facebook is becoming less popular among students. Of course, the survey sample is biased to those that use Facebook already, but these results provide evidence that those who are active on the platform are likely to remain so for some time. The results confirmed anecdotal observations that mobile is by far the preferred platform for Facebook use, with 92 percent of respondents indicating that a mobile device was most often used to check Facebook.

A majority of students (63 percent) expressed some level of discomfort at being targeted with advertising based on their personal information. Many students saw the use of their personal information in this way as unacceptable, although a significant number stated that they did not have a problem with it or saw it as a necessary trade-off. This is further discussed below in our analysis of qualitative comments received.

Perhaps our most significant finding was that far fewer students (34 percent) expressed any level of discomfort with the library targeting them with adverts, and less than 13 percent expressed moderate or extreme discomfort. As illustrated in figure 5.8 below, this is a much lower level of discomfort compared to their feelings on targeted advertising in general. Possible explanations for this observation are that

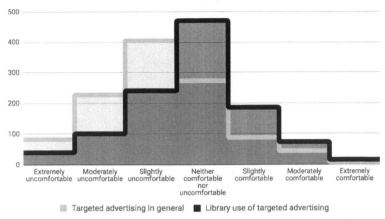

Figure 5.8. Student attitude toward targeted advertising in general versus library use of targeted advertising

the library is seen as a trusted institution or that students believe that their library will target them with messages relevant to them. Further investigation is needed to fully explain this result.

Analysis of Qualitative Comments

Apart from the quantitative survey questions, the survey also allowed respondents to optionally submit free text comments on personal data privacy and advertising/promotional messages on Facebook. We received 122 such comments, and our analysis showed that the comments fell into five broad categories. Twenty-five comments showed **negative attitudes** toward advertising on Facebook, with one commenter even saying, "Don't do that on facebook, it is awful." Twenty-one comments demonstrated a **neutral attitude** to Facebook advertising, such as "as long as my personal information is not sold to other unauthorized and illegal firms for illegal use, I'm ok with that." Twenty-one comments showed a **positive attitude**, indicating that Facebook advertising was useful: "Actually I can accept Facebook using my personal data to filter the news or ads that is suitable for me. That helps me to save more time to search the related Facebook pages for myself."

Most revealing were the final two categories we identified. We received twelve comments **expressing acceptance of the monetization of personal data** on a free platform with an advertising-dependent business model, such as:

- "There's no free lunch in the world, Ads based on personal data would be reasonable costs for using free online services."
- "I am aware that Facebook uses my personal information. Although I don't like it very much, I won't stop using Facebook because of it."

And finally, we received forty-six comments about **personal data privacy and its importance**. Two representative examples:

- "Users are not very clear about how facebook uses their private information."
- "I feel that in this modern society where full of electronic devices and widely excess [sic] to the internet, it is impossible for us to have as much privacy as before if you choose to use any of the social media that are available. Hence, it [sic] a must for us to accept that some of our privacy is being 'stolen', but what we actually have to do is that we must be more careful while surfing the internet and make sure that we are not giving too much details on our privacy such as e banking password and so on on the internet."

Ultimately, the survey results give us confidence going forward in continuing with the use of Facebook advertisements. As in any diverse community, there will be some that oppose the practice. However, our findings here show that the majority of our users are comfortable with their library targeting them with paid promotions on Facebook.

CONCLUSION

This chapter demonstrates how paid Facebook advertising can be part of an overall social media strategy that seeks to engage and connect with audiences online. The results of our recent institutional campaigns show that Facebook advertising can be used to build significant awareness of and engagement with the library at a relatively low cost. The student survey showed that among respondents Facebook use is either remaining constant or increasing and that students are on the whole not averse to the idea of libraries targeting them directly via Facebook advertising. Taken together, these factors underline the potential of targeted Facebook advertising for institutions who are comfortable with the platform, have invested resources in compelling social media content, and are ready to capitalize on their efforts through paid advertising. The wealth of literature about how libraries are using Facebook to interact with their communities, contrasted with the relative dearth of literature about paid Facebook advertising, suggests that targeted paid advertising has yet to be widely explored. We hope that by sharing our experience with Facebook advertising and providing an overview of Facebook Ad Manager, librarians will feel equipped to explore the options available via Facebook advertising to truly make the most of their community-building efforts on social media.

NOTES

1. "Facebook Reports Third Quarter 2016 Results," last modified November 2, 2016, investor.fb.com/investor-news/press-release-details/2016/Facebook-Reports-Third-Quarter -2016-Results/default.aspx.

2. Scott W. H. Young and Doralyn Rossmann, "Building Library Community through Social Media," *Information Technology and Libraries* 34, no. 1, (2015).

3. Joe Phua and S. J. Ahn, "Explicating the 'Like' on Facebook Brand Pages: The Effect of Intensity of Facebook Use, Number of Overall 'Likes', and Number of Friends' 'Likes' on Consumers' Brand," *Journal of Marketing Communications* 22, no. 5 (2014): 545.

4. For more information on how the Facebook News Feed algorithm works, see "How News Feed Works," Facebook Help Center, www.facebook.com/help/32713101403 6297/.

5. Scott W. H. Young, Angela M. Tate, Doralyn Rossmann, and Mary Anne Hansen, "The Social Media Toll Road: The Promise and Peril of Facebook Advertising," *College and Research Library News* 75, no. 8 (2014): 427–34, accessed December 21, 2016, crln.acrl.org/content/75/8/427.full.

6. Christopher Chan, "Your Mileage May Vary: Facebook Advertising Revisited," *College and Research Library News* 77, no. 4 (2016): 190–93, accessed December 21, 2016, crln.acrl.org/content/77/4/190.full.

7. For more on understanding Facebook's pricing structure, see "Understanding How Bidding and Our Ads Auction Work," Facebook Advertiser Help Center, www.facebook.com/business/help/430291176997542.

8. For more information on advertising account permissions, see "What Permissions Are Available When Giving Someone Access to My Advertising Account?" Facebook Advertiser Help Center, www.facebook.com/business/help/155909647811305.

9. For more on how Facebook billing thresholds work, see "When Will I Pay for My Facebook Ads?" Facebook Advertiser Help Center, www.facebook.com/business/help/105373 712886516?helpref=faq_content.

10. Young et al., "The Social Media Toll Road," 427–28.

11. Chan, "Your Mileage May Vary," 191.

12. For more about how Facebook adverts integrate with Instagram, see "Instagram Advertising Basics," Facebook Advertiser Help Center, www.facebook.com/business/help/9762 40832426180.

13. Full dataset available: Christopher Chan and Joanna Hare, "Survey Results: Hong Kong University Student Attitudes towards Targeted Advertising in Facebook," Mendeley Data, v2, 2017. doi: 10.17632/txy2ddfgmv.2

BIBLIOGRAPHY

Chan, Christopher, and Hare, Joanna. "Survey Results: Hong Kong University Student Attitudes towards Targeted Advertising in Facebook." Mendeley Data, v2, 2017.

Chan, Christopher. "Your Mileage May Vary: Facebook Advertising Revisited." *College and Research Library News* 77, no. 4 (2016): 190–93. crln.acrl.org/content/77/4/190.full.

"Facebook Reports Third Quarter 2016 Results." Last modified November 2, 2016. investor.fb.com/investor-news/press-release-details/2016/Facebook-Reports-Third-Quarter-2016-Results/default.aspx.

"How News Feed Works." Facebook Help Center. www.facebook.com/help/32713101403 6297/.

"Instagram Advertising Basics." Facebook Advertiser Help Center. www.facebook.com/busi ness/help/976240832426180.

Phua, Joe, and S. J. Ahn. "Explicating the 'Like' on Facebook Brand Pages: The Effect of Intensity of Facebook Use, Number of Overall 'Likes', and Number of Friends' 'Likes' on Consumers' Brand." *Journal of Marketing Communications* 22, no. 5 (2014): 544–59.

"Understanding How Bidding and Our Ads Auction Work." Facebook Advertiser Help Center. www.facebook.com/business/help/430291176997542.

"What Permissions are Available When Giving Someone Access to My Advertising Account?" Facebook Advertiser Help Center. www.facebook.com/business/help/155909647811305.

"When Will I Pay for My Facebook Ads?" Facebook Advertiser Help Center. www.facebook .com/business/help/105373712886516?helpref=faq_content.

Young, Scott W. H., and Doralyn Rossmann. "Building Library Community through Social Media." *Information Technology and Libraries* 34, no. 1 (2015): 20–37.

Young, Scott W. H., Angela M. Tate, Doralyn Rossmann, and Mary Anne Hansen. "The Social Media Toll Road: The Promise and Peril of Facebook Advertising." *College and Research Library News* 75, no. 8 (2014): 427–34.

II

BUILDING COMMUNITIES
OF LIBRARY PROFESSIONALS

6

Building Communities of Practice in the Library Profession

Katie Elson Anderson

OVERVIEW

One of the many strengths of library professionals is their motivation and ability to identify, create, and nurture communities. Librarians also have a penchant for collaborating, sharing, learning, and teaching. Communities of practice (CoPs) can emerge when these two passions are combined. A CoP, unlike an assigned team or group, is organic and often self-motivated by an interested group of like-minded individuals. This chapter will provide an overview of CoPs while also defining CoPs, with a focus on online communities. The impact and importance of CoPs in the library profession is discussed along with examples of successful CoPs and advice on harnessing their potential among library professionals.

THE BEGINNINGS OF ONLINE COMMUNITIES OF PRACTICE

My first job upon graduating from college with a degree in anthropology (with a focus on archaeology—thank you, Dr. Jones) was evening supervisor in a small business library. The year was 1994; e-mails came via Pine[1]; Webcrawler,[2] the first fully indexed search engine, was used to view pages on the World Wide Web; and a terminal had just appeared at the circulation desk for checkouts with the newly implemented electronic catalog. Evenings in the library were sometimes slow, and once my work for the day was complete, I spent some time exploring the new worlds opened up by the developing technology of the mid-1990s. While it may have appeared to those on the other side of the desk that I was working intently on an important project, in reality I was discovering the many online newsgroups and communities accessed via Usenet.

In 1994 Usenet was not new, but it was becoming more accessible as the technology became more mainstream. Usenet was first conceived in 1979 as a network of computers that would link a community of Unix programmers and users.[3] It soon expanded to host newsgroups and discussion forums, and a statement of policy was proposed in 1981 that indicated the importance of Usenet being a public access network and stated, "All users are to be given access to all newsgroups except that private newsgroups can be created which are protected."[4] The early 1990s marked increased access to this technology, thus expanding Usenet's reach beyond programmers and to users who shared a desire to discuss ideas on a variety of topics, which included war, peace, politics, science, technology, philosophy, ethics, science fiction, and literature. The excitement and potential of a system that allowed computer users to connect around specific topics and interests is evident in a quote from the 1997 book *Netizens: On the History and Impact of Usenet and the Internet*: "So welcome to the world of Usenet. Something very special is happening, and it is one of the most important achievements of the twentieth century."[5]

While I was using this very important achievement for reading alt.food.taco-bell to learn about the wonders of the seven-layer burrito and odes to sporks, librarians were bringing Usenet to the attention of their colleagues. A 1994 article by Polly and Cisler[6] provides a brief history and description of Usenet as well as details the primary hierarchies that attempted to categorize the thousands of topics being discussed. The article suggests that reference librarians need to be aware of the groups of Usenet in order to include them in their resources and notes that Usenet is an "Internet resource more of us in libraries need to read, contribute to and use."[7]

It was not until I began researching and engaging with social media as a librarian that I began to think more about those early days of Usenet groups. The social media site Reddit (reddit.com) immediately reminded me of those early newsgroups, and sure enough, the Taco Bell appreciation continues in the subreddit at www.reddit.com/r/tacobell/. This means that for more than twenty years individuals have been coming together online and creating a community around a fast-food restaurant chain and its menu items. The technology has changed, but the gathering of individuals around specific interests to create a community has not. Even an early lamentation on Usenet could be applied to many social media sites today: "Unfortunately, the incredibly heavy traffic and the contentious nature of some of the participants have kept librarians from making use of this huge body of volatile information and opinion."[8] The necessity of librarians to use and understand the technology that creates, supports, and encourages CoPs remains unchanged. While the Taco Bell example is a humorous and not exactly practical example of the development of online CoPs, it does show the evolution of these virtual communities since the early days of the Internet and set the stage for viewing today's social media sites as CoPs.

THE HISTORY OF COMMUNITIES OF PRACTICE

Three years before I spent my evenings reading stories of denied two-dollar bills at Taco Bell,[9] Lave and Wenger are credited with defining the concept of CoPs. In their study on apprenticeships and learning as a situational activity, they describe what they call legitimate peripheral participation. In describing this concept, they look at the process by which "learners inevitably participate in communities of practitioners."[10] They go on to describe a CoP as a "set of relations among persons, activity and world, over time and in relation with other tangential and overlapping communities of practice."[11] This original definition of CoP was expanded by Wenger in his 1998 publication *Communities of Practice* and again in 2002.[12] Continued exploration of the concept of learning as a social participation led to the 2002 definition of CoPs as "groups of people who share a concern or a passion for something they do and learn how to do it better as they interact regularly."[13] The definition has been interpreted and expanded, but the basic components as established by Wenger remain consistent in most cases.

CoPs are largely informal and organic, developing around a specific interest or pursuit. While there are certainly examples of communities of practice that are created with specific goals and membership, more often these CoPs are grassroots efforts by like-minded individuals who share a common pursuit, interest, or profession. Most definitions of CoPs emphasize their distinction from teams or groups. While CoPs do share a set of communal resources, procedures, rituals, and specific idioms similar to teams, CoPs have not been assigned tasks or resources and are largely self-motivated. Formal teams and groups are often developed in order to complete a specific task. The primary function of CoPs is for learning; they provide individuals with a collaborative space for learning outside of classrooms, training rooms, and offices. For the purposes of this chapter, which focuses on the use of CoPs in the library profession, we will use this definition:

> Communities of practice are collaborative, informal networks that support professional practitioners in their efforts to develop shared understandings and engage in work-relevant knowledge building.[14]

A CoP should not be imposed but rather grown. Hara identifies the seven actions as described by Wenger that could be taken in order to cultivate CoPs:

1. A community should be designed so that it can evolve naturally.
2. Opportunities for the establishment of an open dialogue between inside and outside perspectives should be established.
3. A community should allow for different levels of participation.
4. Room for development of both public and private community spaces should be accommodated.
5. The focus of the community should be on the value of the community.

6. A combination of familiarity and excitement should be cultivated.
7. The community should establish a regular rhythm for the community.[15]

This should not be taken as a step-by-step guide for the creation of a CoP but rather as a set of guidelines as to how one might be cultivated.

Along with the characteristics described in the guidelines, there are three components to a CoP: domain, community, and practice. According to Wenger, a CoP has an identity defined by a shared domain of interest. This makes a CoP different from a group of friends or network of professionals because the membership implies a commitment to the domain. The shared interests and understandings of that domain are what codify the community. This community as defined by Wenger is a place where members engage in joint activities and discussions, help each other, and share information, the distinction being that the members of a CoP learn from each other and interact with each other, engaging in joint activities, discussions, and sharing. A group of people making up a community that do not establish relationships around learning, teaching, and sharing is not considered a CoP. The final component is the practice—members of a CoP must be practitioners who "develop a shared repertoire of resources including experiences, stories, tools, ways of addressing recurring problems—in short, a shared practice."[16] Wenger points out that this takes time and sustained interaction.

The key to this sustained interaction is engagement and motivation from the community. The participants of CoPs are able to share their creativity and innovation with mutually engaged and motivated participants; it is the connection of the participants that distinguishes a CoP from a group. An effective CoP is one where knowledge is shared, supported, and sustained. The relationships of trust are key to the success of the community. While relationships are key to the dynamic of a CoP, those relationships do not necessarily have to always be positive. As Wenger says, "Peace, happiness and harmony are therefore not necessary properties of a community of practice."[17] This is important for members of the community to remember, especially in larger communities with less specific domains, which are more subject to personal bias, promotion, and controversial topics that to some may fall outside of the community's domain. While the expectation of a successful CoP should be one of mutual engagement and respect, there may not always be agreement, consensus, or guaranteed civility.

Relationship-based CoPs were around long before the term was coined. Humans have been learning and sharing across organizational and geographic boundaries for ages. They began as face-to-face meetings and have grown with technology to include entirely virtual CoPs. Some of the earliest virtual CoPs were listservs and Usenet groups, which continue to be actively engaged today. Social media platforms have expanded the opportunities for virtual CoPs, providing robust places for sharing of knowledge and professional development. Belzowski states that "the fact that they exist as a natural structure for people who wish to share and collaborate using knowledge as a commodity to achieve a common purpose, makes them even more potent as a deliberate management tool."[18]

The literature on CoPs is fairly extensive and interdisciplinary. Business and organizational literature refers to the concept as "knowledge management" while others may describe them in the context of a "personal learning network." (See chapter 7 for a full discussion of personal learning networks.) A brief overview of the literature with a library and educational focus reveals that CoPs are recognized as important to the education and professional development of library professionals. Belzowski et al.[19] identify CoPs as promising tools to develop and sustain professional identity. There is an emphasis on how CoPs can be tools to build professional empathy through meaningful connections and improved perception, giving librarians a sense of belonging and sense of shared purpose. In their discussion on the role of educators, practitioners, professional associations, and employing organizations in mentoring and creating informational professionals, Reynolds et al. emphasize the need for "libraries of all types in all sectors to employ and nurture informational professionals who are passionate, engaged contributors to their profession and to society."[20] Their discussions include the use of CoPs for nurturing professionals in "learning to be" or acquiring the attributes of a professional: enculturation into the profession.

Additional articles on CoPs and libraries focus on specific types of libraries. Oguz looked at technology adoption decisions in digital libraries and found that respondents to their survey "indicated that CoPs provided them with a rich and creative learning environment where they were able to gain considerably from diverse skills, ideas and perspectives available in CoPs to meet organization goals."[21] Bilodeau and Carson look at the role of CoPs in the professional education of academic librarians, finding that "the conceptual model of communities of practice produces a useful perspective for understanding the learning of librarians and for designing a library school experience that is more effective in preparing students for their future careers as librarians."[22] Burns et al. examine CoPs in school library education. Focusing on Wenger's three elements of belonging—engagement, alignment, and imagination—they look at how distance education provides insights into the way emerging school librarians develop their CoPs. They conclude that these CoPs "assist in shaping their identities and collaborative pedagogies through guided support from more experienced school library teacher educators."[23] Novakovich et al. address the challenge of incorporating social media skills and identity in virtual CoPs into a curriculum. They note that "classrooms often fail to transfer the skills that are required for practicing communication" and discuss CoPs in that context.[24] Nistor and Fisher test a quantitative model for looking at CoPs in academia.[25] Oguz et al. focus on collaborating through CoPs in the digital age, focusing on virtual, Web 2.0 technologies such as social media for supporting CoPs.[26] Kim focuses on integrating CoPs into library services and explores the "implication that community of practice suggests for libraries and the role that librarians can take to foster communities of practice."[27] The article includes implications for all types of libraries for fostering CoPs.

LIBRARIES FOSTERING COMMUNITIES OF PRACTICE

Libraries by their nature are incubators of CoPs. They are physical spaces for participants to gather in order to share interests, resources, and ideas. As central and community institutions, they can serve as focal points for practitioners from all areas; storytellers, quilters, readers, writers, parents, teens can all use the library space and resources to form their own CoPs. Libraries are excellent spaces for the growth and nurturing of CoPs. The fostering of CoPs can be as simple as providing space for an in-person meeting of a CoP or more complicated such as setting up virtual spaces for academic librarians and faculty to engage. Libraries can teach individuals how to use the virtual platforms that can be used for CoPs through both formal and informal instruction. In many cases, librarians may not even realize that they are fostering CoPs; because so much of what libraries and librarians do emphasizes community and engagement, it is almost not even a separate concept. For example, helping a knitter through the technical steps to join ravelry.com and providing a brief introduction to this knitting CoP is an example of fostering a CoP. Helping a homeschooling parent find online groups that create and share curriculum is providing that parent access to a CoP. Formal trainings on the social media platforms that are used to cultivate CoPs are also important parts of how libraries and librarians can foster CoPs. By introducing and explaining social media platforms such as Facebook and Twitter, librarians are providing patrons with the tools to engage with other motivated individuals around shared passions. Academic librarians can foster CoPs by providing spaces for campus-wide stakeholders to meet, mentoring new library professionals, instructing students, and collaborating with departmental faculty. Academic libraries can provide both informal and formal trainings on the online tools and technologies that will help others participate in and create CoPs. By supporting these online tools for instruction, organization, and storage of resources, training, and forums, academic libraries can foster and help others foster CoPs. Instruction and trainings can also provide a feeling of confidence in these tools, allowing learners to begin to grow their own CoPs.

   Kim provides five stages of development for CoPs: potential, coalescing, maturing, stewardship, and transformation. There is a place for libraries in each of these stages. The first stage of potential involves determining people who have common interests around the same domain while identifying possible coordinators and leaders. The coalescing of a CoP takes place as those identified develop relationships and trust by establishing the community's activities and spaces. As the CoP matures, it begins to manage boundaries and organize knowledge before it moves on to stewardship, where it must maintain engagement and vitality. Eventually the CoP will transform with new ideas, goals, and relationships; split into separate groups with different foci; or even just cease as a CoP.

Libraries and librarians can play an important role in growing and maintaining CoPs. As places of knowledge, sharing, education, and learning, libraries can be more active in their roles of sharing knowledge and providing collaborative learning through CoPs. Kim goes on to point out that "by adopting the notion of Community of Practice, libraries will be able to widen their roles as cultural and educational institutions."[28] A librarian's role in a CoP will vary according to the domain, but generally the librarian can share knowledge and expertise, make connections, provide context, instruct, and assist in problem solving.

Kim provides the following list of ways that librarians can contribute to the successful performance of CoPs:

- Provide access to the existing body of knowledge that is relevant to the knowledge domain that the CoP focuses on.
- Validate the authenticity of the knowledge resources.
- Add value to the knowledge resources by providing them with context.
- Capture, organize, and disseminate knowledge resources created by the community members in the form of both documents and narratives.
- Develop the optimal taxonomies of the knowledge domain to organize knowledge created and collected by the community members, thus enabling effective knowledge flow throughout the organization.
- Provide efficient tools for searching and browsing knowledge repositories.
- Facilitate the contribution of knowledge resources from the members of the CoP.
- Ensure that knowledge resources added by the community members are continually updated.
- Support situated learning among the participants of CoPs.
- Teach them information literacy skills.
- Provide engaging social spaces for the gatherings and activities of CoPs. The spaces can be provided both online and offline.[29]

PROFESSIONAL COMMUNITIES OF PRACTICE

Librarians have been engaging in CoPs since long before the advent of social media platforms. While I was reading about tacos back in the 1990s, librarians had already been sharing, gathering, and motivating via listservs and Usenet groups. Librarians as a profession are quick to embrace and experiment with new technologies, and the professional CoPs that exist today are evidence of this. The following is a brief overview of some of the active CoPs for librarians on the social media platforms that best serve the needs of virtual CoPs. The domains range from simply "being a librarian" to more focused interests within and even without (knitting! cats!) the profession.

Facebook

The nature of CoPs is that they grow organically. They are usually started by a few interested participants who spread the word by inviting members. Those members then invite more people and the community grows. Facebook is an excellent platform for this model of creation using either pages or groups. Anyone can create Facebook pages and groups and invite members to like or join them. Different privacy settings allow for more private CoPs, though in many cases the more open the CoP, the more likely the group will attract mutual engaged practitioners. The Facebook page format allows for posting, commenting, and sharing of files and media. Thus, it is conducive to meeting the creation of content and sharing of ideas, an important element of CoPs.

A search on Facebook for pages and groups with the word "library" or "librarian" provides hundreds of results. These groups range from small local groups to large international groups. Many of them can easily be considered communities of practice as the members engage around a common interest, solve problems, create content, and share ideas. In looking at the variety of CoPs on Facebook, one can observe librarians asking questions, offering solutions, collaborating on creative and innovative ideas, and so on. Highlighted below are just some of the available librarian CoPs on Facebook:

- ALA Think Tank (www.facebook.com/groups/ALAthinkTANK/)
- Libraries and Social Media (www.facebook.com/groups/LibrarySocial/)
- Library Marketing and Outreach (ACRL) (www.facebook.com/groups/acrl.lmao/)
- Library Employees Support Network (www.facebook.com/groups/toxic.libraries/)
- Library Management Group (www.facebook.com/groups/1524906657799350/)

If you are looking to connect with library professionals via Facebook, a good way to start is to join a community listed above or identify one of the many more that exist. Many times, smaller, more specialized groups are formed out of a larger group. For example, a Library Pokémon Go Support group was started by librarians discussing the specifics of the app on a different librarian page. The potential for a CoP dedicated to the app was identified, and so a CoP focused exclusively on the Pokémon Go app, specifically in the context of libraries, was created. Once you have joined a Facebook group, you are likely to discover other ones that are mentioned in the group. Another way to find groups specific to your interests and profession is to search either the Groups or Pages with library-related terms. Depending on the privacy settings of the group, you may need to await approval from a moderator.

Twitter

Unlike Facebook, Twitter does not have a mechanism for creating groups. Instead, CoPs emerge primarily via hashtags. A hashtag can create both a synchronous and asynchronous CoP. (See chapter 9 for a full discussion of the #critlib CoP.) By following the hashtags, one can join in the conversation and identify practitioners who share the domain. Members of the CoP can share ideas, documents, and media, albeit with the 140-character limitation. Hashtags can be temporary, based around a specific event such as a conference, which would create a more transient CoP than more established hashtags. These established hashtags are usually ongoing conversations among practitioners, though some have specific days and times where more synchronous discussion takes place, and they range from more formal discussions of new trends to the more lighthearted #saturdaylibrarian sharing of weekend librarian experiences. Some examples of active CoPs on Twitter use the following hashtags:

- #libchat
- #uklibchat
- #inaljchat
- #LISPROCHAT
- #critlib
- #edchat
- #infolit
- #edtech
- #saturdaylibrarian
- #tlchat

There are many more hashtags that discuss libraries, community, education, and just about any topic you can imagine. Searching on Twitter for keywords of interest can lead one to these specific hashtags, or lists of these are also available on the web. When deciding to start a CoP using Twitter, it is important to create a hashtag that does not take up too many of the precious 140 characters.

Reddit

Similar to the original Usenet format, Reddit provides a place, or subreddit, for practitioners to gather around a single domain. While a much smaller community than Facebook or Twitter, Reddit does have several CoPs that may be relevant to librarians. Reddit can be much more anonymous than Facebook and thus individuals may feel more comfortable posting more sensitive questions, especially when it comes to job seeking or managing advice. These include:

- www.reddit.com/r/Libraries/
- www.reddit.com/r/Library/

- www.reddit.com/r/LibraryDisplays/
- www.reddit.com/r/books/
- www.reddit.com/r/Archivists/

A keyword search is helpful in locating subreddits that focus on a particular interest. Reddit is known at times for NSFW (Not Safe for Work) content, so a user should be prepared, especially when venturing into CoPs outside of the library and education focus. For more in-depth information regarding Reddit and its applications in libraries, see the author's article "Ask Me Anything: What Is Reddit?"[30]

Slack

I first became aware of Slack when the editors for this book suggested that the contributors use this platform in order to stay connected during the process of creating this book's content. The Slack channel for this book provided a place for multiple conversations based around a single domain, the book. Slack can be defined as an Enterprise Networking System, which is essentially a social networking platform that is used primarily in businesses. This is not to say that Slack is only for businesses, just that it is the primary target market. The platform centers around a team concept in an attempt to streamline communication among multiple groups. It employs the use of hashtags and "channels" to organize communication, as well as the ability to tag other users employing the @ sign. This allows for small-group discussion within the larger community when necessary. Slack provides easy ways to share documents and create a repertoire while allowing for both lurking and engagement. Since it was created specifically for team building, there are some additional features such as icebreaker apps and other community-building tools that are both entertaining and functional. Generally, a Slack channel is created for a specific group or community and then members are invited to join. There are some open communities that can be joined by searching on terms such as "education," "library," and so forth as well. My article "Getting Acquainted with Social Networks and Apps: Picking Up Slack in Communication and Collaboration"[31] provides more details about this app and its potential for librarians.

Other CoP platforms

There are other platforms where CoPs can thrive, depending on the motivation and engagement of the users. When Google+ first started, several different communities of librarians formed, creating CoPs. While these still exist, engagement overall with Google+ was not embraced, thus diminishing the impact of these CoPs. Examples of other virtual spaces where the elements of CoPs are apparent include Goodreads, LinkedIn, and Slideshare. Previously popular places like MySpace and Second Life illustrate that practitioners will find the spaces in which to virtually convene around shared interests.

Librarians will benefit from taking part in these CoPs for their own professional development and networking opportunities. An additional benefit of knowing the platforms and their potential is being able to direct patrons to these CoPs as part of providing library services.

CREATING, NURTURING, EDUCATING: LIBRARIANS AND COMMUNITIES OF PRACTICE

Libraries and librarians are valuable to the creation and maintenance of CoPs. Social media platforms provide the tools for librarians to harness the collaborative, communicative, instructional, and engaging power of CoPs both internally and externally. Engagement with patrons via social media sites creates a CoP with the library and its resources, activities, and so forth as domain. A common question for librarians and libraries using social media is whether engagement is happening with the intended audience, which is generally thought to be the patrons. It is important to remember that engagement among libraries and librarians through social media should not be overlooked because this too is an important CoP. The voices in this book are just a few of the librarians who have worked to create, innovate, sustain, and promote CoPs through social media. Librarians who embraced social media early on were often one of the few in their geographic locations experimenting with it and learning about it. Finding others with the same interest became essential in order to grow and learn. CoPs began to organically sprout as like-minded librarians found each other on Facebook, Twitter, and other social media platforms. Librarians quickly recognized the tool as a way to engage and connect with others using those tools in order to enhance their own understanding and potential of the tool. The editors and authors of this book found and know each other through one of the many professional CoPs that exist. The editors and authors of this book were able to create a CoP for the book itself, sharing, learning, and motivating through Slack, Google Hangouts, Google Docs, and other methods of communication. The experience of writing this chapter was enhanced by knowing that the authors and editors were an available CoP.

There are, of course, limitations to CoPs. Belzowski points out that "degrees of power, issues of trust, member preferences and predispositions, size and spatial reach, cultural lack of sense of community, and the pace of change"[32] can all lead to tensions within CoPs. However, CoPs are not guaranteed to be harmonious, and in some ways the tensions can actually assist with problem solving and trust building. It is important, however, to be aware that the experience within a CoP may not always be one without stress or conflict.

Knowing the importance and function of a CoP within libraries and among librarians, it is strongly encouraged that professionals at all stages explore and engage with CoPs. One may even be motivated to create their own when a need is seen, and it is my hope that this chapter has provided enough of an overview for interested parties to create, engage with, and assist in maintaining a CoP. A successful CoP hinges on the relationships and motivation of the practitioners. Libraries and librarians are proven creators and sustainers of communities, both physical and virtual, and thus excellent examples of the creators, sustainers, and users of CoPs.

NOTES

1. "Pine Project History," University of Washington, accessed February 2, 2017, www.washington.edu/pine/overview/project-history.html.

2. "About Webcrawler," Webcrawler, accessed January 31, 2017, www.webcrawler.com/support/aboutus?qc=web&aid=605e630a-0972-4731-a506-23b3045c1d30&ridx=2#history.

3. Michael Hauben and Ronda Hauben, *Netizens: On the History and Impact of Usenet and the Internet* (Los Alamitos, CA: IEEE Computer Society Press, 1997), 39.

4. Hauben and Hauben, *Netizens*, 175.

5. Hauben and Hauben, *Netizens*, 64.

6. Jean Armour Polly and Steve Cisler, "Usenet for Librarians," *Library Journal* 119, no. 15 (1994): 31–32.

7. Polly and Cisler, "Usenet for Librarians," 31.

8. Polly and Cisler, "Usenet for Librarians," 31.

9. David Mikkelson, "Taco Bell Refuses $2 Bill," Snopes, accessed February 5, 2017, www.snopes.com/business/money/tacobell.asp.

10. Jean Lave and Etienne Wenger, *Situated Learning: Legitimate Peripheral Participation* (Cambridge: Cambridge University Press), 1991.

11. Lave and Wenger, *Situated Learning*, 29.

12. Etienne Wenger, *Communities of Practice: Learning, Meaning, and Identity* (New York: Cambridge University Press), 1998; Etienne Wenger, Richard Arnold McDermott, and William Snyder, *Cultivating Communities of Practice: A Guide to Managing Knowledge* (Boston: Harvard Business Press), 2002.

13. Wenger et al., *Cultivating Communities of Practice*, 4.

14. Noriko Hara, *Communities of Practice: Fostering Peer-to-Peer Learning and Informal Knowledge Sharing in the Work Place* (Berlin: Springer Science & Business Media, 2008), 3.

15. Hara, *Communities of Practice*, 4.

16. Etienne Wenger-Trayner and Beverly Wenger-Trayner, "Introduction to Communities of Practice," accessed February 6, 2017, wenger-trayner.com/introduction-to-communities-of-practice/.

17. Wenger, *Communities of Practice*, 77.

18. Nora J. Belzowski, Parker Ladwig, and Thurston Miller, "Crafting Identity, Collaboration, and Relevance for Academic Librarians Using Communities of Practice," *Collaborative Librarianship* 5, no. 1 (2013): 7.

19. Belzowski, Ladwig, and Miller, "Crafting Identity," 2.

20. Sue Reynolds, Mary Carroll, and Bernadette Welch, "Engaging with Our Future: The Role of Educators, Practitioners, Professional Associations and Employing Organisations in the Co-Creation of Information Professionals," *The Australian Library Journal* 65, no. 4 (2016): 318.

21. Fatih Oguz, "Organizational Influences in Technology Adoption Decisions: A Case Study of Digital Libraries," *College & Research Libraries* 77, no. 3 (2016): 328–29.

22. Edward Bilodeau and Pamela Carson, "The Role of Communities of Practice in the Professional Education of Academic Librarians," *Education for Information* 31, nos. 1, 2 (2015): 25.

23. Elizabeth A. Burns, Jody K. Howard, and Sue C. Kimmel, "Development of Communities of Practice in School Library Education," *Journal of Education for Library and Information Science* 57, no. 2 (2016): 109.

24. Jeanette Novakovich, Sophia Miah, and Steven Shaw, "Designing Curriculum to Shape Professional Social Media Skills and Identity in Virtual Communities of Practice," *Computers & Education* 104 (2017): 88.

25. Nicolae Nistor and Frank Fischer, "Communities of Practice in Academia: Testing a Quantitative Model," *Learning, Culture and Social Interaction* 1, no. 2 (2012).

26. Fatih Oguz, Corrie V. Marsh, and Cliff Landis, "Collaboration through Communities of Practice in the Digital Age," in *International Symposium on Information Management in a Changing World* (Berlin: Springer Berlin Heidelberg, 2010), 18–30.

27. Jong Kim, "Integrating Communities of Practice into Library Services," *Collaborative Librarianship* 7, no. 2 (2016): 47.

28. Kim, "Integrating Communities of Practice," 49.

29. Kim, "Integrating Communities of Practice," 52.

30. Katie Elson Anderson, "Ask Me Anything: What Is Reddit?" *Library Hi Tech News* 32, no. 5 (2015): 8–11.

31. Katie Elson Anderson, "Getting Acquainted with Social Networks and Apps: Picking Up the Slack in Communication and Collaboration," *Library Hi Tech News* 33, no. 9 (2016).

32. Belzowski, Ladwig, and Miller, "Crafting Identity."

BIBLIOGRAPHY

"About Webcrawler." Webcrawler. Accessed January 31, 2017. www.webcrawler.com/support/aboutus?qc=web&aid=605e630a-0972-4731-a506-23b3045c1d30&ridx=2#history.

Anderson, Katie Elson. "Ask Me Anything: What Is Reddit?" *Library Hi Tech News* 32, no. 5 (2015): 8–11.

———. "Getting Acquainted with Social Networks and Apps: Picking Up the Slack in Communication and Collaboration." *Library Hi Tech News* 33, no. 9 (2016).

Belzowski, Nora J., Parker Ladwig, and Thurston Miller. "Crafting Identity, Collaboration, and Relevance for Academic Librarians Using Communities of Practice." *Collaborative Librarianship* 5, no. 1 (2013).

Bilodeau, Edward, and Pamela Carson. "The Role of Communities of Practice in the Professional Education of Academic Librarians." *Education for Information* 31, nos. 1, 2 (2015): 25–51.

Burns, Elizabeth A., Jody K. Howard, and Sue C. Kimmel. "Development of Communities of Practice in School Library Education." *Journal of Education for Library and Information Science* 57, no. 2 (2016): 101–11.

Hara, Noriko. *Communities of Practice: Fostering Peer-to-Peer Learning and Informal Knowledge Sharing in the Work Place.* Berlin: Springer Science & Business Media, 2008.

Hauben, Michael, and Ronda Hauben. *Netizens: On the History and Impact of Usenet and the Internet.* Los Alamitos, CA: IEEE Computer Society Press, 1997.

Kim, Jong. "Integrating Communities of Practice into Library Services." *Collaborative Librarianship* 7, no. 2 (2016): 47–55.

Lave, Jean, and Etienne Wenger. *Situated Learning: Legitimate Peripheral Participation.* Cambridge: Cambridge University Press, 1991.

Mikkelson, David. "Taco Bell Refuses $2 Bill." Snopes. Accessed February 5, 2017. www .snopes.com/business/money/tacobell.asp.

Nistor, Nicolae, and Frank Fischer. "Communities of Practice in Academia: Testing a Quantitative Model." *Learning, Culture and Social Interaction* 1, no. 2 (2012): 114–26.

Novakovich, Jeanette, Sophia Miah, and Steven Shaw. "Designing Curriculum to Shape Professional Social Media Skills and Identity in Virtual Communities of Practice." *Computers & Education* 104 (2017): 65–90.

Oguz, Fatih. "Organizational Influences in Technology Adoption Decisions: A Case Study of Digital Libraries." *College & Research Libraries* 77, no. 3 (2016): 314–34.

Oguz, Fatih, Corrie V. Marsh, and Cliff Landis. "Collaboration through Communities of Practice in the Digital Age." In *International Symposium on Information Management in a Changing World.* Berlin: Springer Berlin Heidelberg, 2010, 18–30.

"Pine Project History." University of Washington. Accessed February 2, 2017. www.washing ton.edu/pine/overview/project-history.html.

Polly, Jean Armour, and Steve Cisler. "Usenet for Librarians." *Library Journal* 119, no. 15 (1994): 31–32.

Reynolds, Sue, Mary Carroll, and Bernadette Welch. "Engaging with Our Future: The Role of Educators, Practitioners, Professional Associations and Employing Organisations in the Co-Creation of Information Professionals." *The Australian Library Journal* 65, no. 4 (2016): 317–27.

Wenger, Etienne. *Communities of Practice: Learning, Meaning, and Identity.* New York: Cambridge University Press, 1998.

Wenger, Etienne, Richard Arnold McDermott, and William Snyder. *Cultivating Communities of Practice: A Guide to Managing Knowledge.* Boston: Harvard Business Press, 2002.

Wenger-Trayner, Etienne, and Beverly Wenger-Trayner. "Introduction to Communities of Practice." Accessed February 6, 2017. wenger-trayner.com/introduction-to-communities-of-practice/.

7

Building a Personal Learning Network

Stony Evans

OVERVIEW

Social media is a wonderful resource for sharing and connecting others to information. The global connectivity that the Internet and social media provide librarians is an amazing resource that many of us probably fail to fully use in our daily work routines. This chapter will focus on how the development of a personal learning network (PLN) completely changed my practices as a high school teacher librarian. A PLN has given me access to library and education professionals that I have never had before. It has also helped me learn about new techniques and resources for librarianship. I continue to see that librarians, regardless of what type, work to connect people, technology, and information. After reading this chapter, you should gain the basics to begin growing your own PLN.

PERSONAL LEARNING NETWORK: TOOLS

Twitter

Probably one of the most significant changes in my career occurred a few years ago when one of my supervisors helped me to better understand Twitter. Prior to this, I had attended a few professional conference sessions on Twitter, but I really didn't see its significance in education. Only 140 characters certainly didn't seem like enough to communicate much value, and the hashtags really didn't make much sense. Then one of my supervising principals explained to me that Twitter education chats were great places to learn and network with other educators. An education chat is essentially a hashtag that a group of educators monitor at a specific time (or times) each week. There are Twitter chats happening all over the country and world at any given hour.

One of the first chats I monitored was #tlchat[1] (teacher librarian chat). Since I really didn't understand how information was exchanged at first, I simply found what time the chat was scheduled to meet. Then I lurked and watched the discussion. It was amazing to me to see practitioners posting questions and exchanging thoughts in only 140 characters. It was like attending a library conference since everyone was so eager to learn and share information. After watching a few of these events, I finally built up the nerve to respond to some of the questions posted by chat moderators. When I responded, several participants favorited or retweeted my messages. In addition, many followed me at the end of the chat session. If they were an educator or librarian, I followed them back. This activity went on for several months, and during that time my PLN grew by hundreds. Later, my network grew to the thousands. Each person in that growing network was a passionate and knowledgeable professional. During the week, I would participate in chat sessions with educators all over the country. Some of these people were administrators, authors, technology specialists, and even business leaders. I discovered there was something to learn from virtually every type of chat. It is fascinating because I began to see a lot of the same individuals in the sessions each week. It became normal to feel as if I knew some of the people in the sessions even though we had never met in person.

One of the biggest benefits that I began to realize is that I had instant access to a nationwide PLN at any time of the day. There were a few times I would post questions about technology or other education-related issues to a specific hashtag (like #tlchat), and nearly every time I would receive a response. Another benefit I started to notice is that Twitter chat sessions had a similar energy to that generated by attending a professional conference session. I would come out of chat sessions excited about things I had learned, and I would be ready to return to school the next day.

Facebook

I started using Facebook in 2009, and at that time it was primarily a tool for connecting with family, friends from high school and college, and former students. Through the use of Twitter, my national and international PLN has now begun to overflow into Facebook. I have also been invited to Facebook groups that are primarily about school librarianship and/or librarianship. This has provided an additional opportunity to connect with others. Facebook has allowed me to share photos, videos, and blog posts with PLN friends that I have never met around the country and world. In fact, it has given me access to some of the thought leaders in my field in a way not previously possible. I can see what they are posting on their Facebook pages, and they can view my posts. This has allowed interaction and collaboration that helped my career as a school librarian. Through Facebook groups, users can network regionally, nationally, and internationally. Facebook is familiar to most social media users and it is easy to share thoughts, links to webpages, photos, and videos that resonate with your community.

Instagram

I began using Instagram about two years ago. There are now more school, public, and academic libraries using Instagram than when I started. I see the same trend in that some thought leaders in our profession are constantly posting photos and video clips on this network much as they do on Facebook. The same hashtags are used on both Twitter and Instagram. I've also noticed that Facebook is using some of these same hashtags. This has allowed me to find some of my Twitter and Facebook PLN colleagues on Instagram. I am curious to see how this network continues to develop and the connections that come from it.

Blogging

I decided to start a school library blog in March 2014. I had already been experimenting with some social media by sharing photos and information about our many library programs. Blogging just seemed like another way to share the value of our library with the learning community. There are many free blogging platforms available on the web. In considering which platform to use, I looked at Blogger, WordPress, and Weebly. All of these offered similar options and features. I created Library Media Tech Talk[2] using Google's Blogger. At first, I mainly blogged about conferences I attended and our collaborative library programs. By 2016, blogging had become a weekly practice for me. It is a powerful reflective tool that helps me improve my teaching practices.

Over the course of nearly three years, the Library Media Tech Talk blog has allowed me to connect with countless librarians (including the editors of this book). While attending conferences, I have discovered that some school library thought leaders have read some of my articles. Blogging allows us to share ideas with the world, *instantly*. We never know who may read our thoughts and stories. The blog started with mainly parents and colleagues reading the material. Now I get messages from people across our state, nation, and world. The blog has provided connections with people I would have never met in person. It is a powerful way to share the value of the library. It is truly a living resume that one can build upon each time he or she chooses to contribute another article.

Mystery Skype and Mystery Hangouts

Through my PLN Twitter education chats, I learned about Mystery Skype and Mystery Hangouts. If you are not familiar with these games, they are worth investigating. The basic idea is to connect your class with another class or individual via webcam. Neither class will know where the other is located. Each participant must use questioning techniques (with *yes* or *no* responses) to determine the location of the opponent first. By connecting via webcam, we give students an opportunity to build a community outside of the school walls. In addition, I have added new educator friends to my PLN by connecting to these activities and regularly keep in touch with many of these new friends.

In 2015, we tried our first Mystery Skype with an eighth-grade social studies class in the library. It was one of the most exciting activities I have ever witnessed. The students were all engaged the entire period. They were having fun, and they were learning in the library. Our first state to connect with was Maine. I immediately wrote a blog article about the event, and it wasn't long until more schools were reaching out to me for Mystery Skype/Mystery Hangouts. Because of the instant sharing of information on social media, I was able to learn about this activity. It changed my thinking since it helped us tear down the walls of the school with a simple webcam. This led to numerous additional Mystery Skypes/Mystery Hangouts in many different classes.

We have also discovered that Skype and Google Hangouts allow us to connect regularly with other schools and colleagues. It provides an additional opportunity to extend the PLN.

Other Tools

Each week there are many different education chats occurring around the country. I have already mentioned learning about Mystery Skype and Mystery Hangouts on social media. To illustrate other benefits waiting to be discovered within social media PLNs, I will share some specific tools I have learned about in recent months.

One of my international educator friends is Àngels Soriano. She lives in Valencia, Spain, and the two of us first connected on Twitter in 2015. Àngels introduced me to a Microsoft product called Skype Translator. We have used it to communicate many times this year. We have a language barrier since Àngels speaks Spanish and I speak English. The tool allows us to translate our language into another in real time. I learned about Skype Translator much faster due to Àngels being in my PLN. It has helped me be a better teacher librarian and connector in my school.

Another example of a tool I learned about through my PLN is Voxer. It is an app that allows users to exchange voice messages. It has been a great way for me to connect with my PLN in a more personal way. My PLN friend Lynn Kleinmeyer told me about Voxer. After I installed the app, Lynn and I were able to hear each other's voices in our weekly message exchanges. Lynn is a public school teacher librarian in Iowa, and the two of us frequently collaborate. Voxer has allowed us to brainstorm together. I have also used Voxer with other members of my PLN.

There are two other examples of trending educational tools I have been exposed to by my Twitter PLN. One is Minecraft Education Edition. This is a game that allows users to virtually build anything in a video game format. I have seen it discussed on Microsoft Education social media networks. Another tool is Digital Breakout

EDU. The Breakout EDU concept is essentially bringing an escape room game to the classroom. It involves purchasing a Breakout box with several different types of locks. The purpose is to present content through a series of puzzles that participants must use teamwork skills to solve. The end goal is to solve all puzzles and open all locks. For individuals that do not wish to purchase the box and locks, they can use the Digital Breakout EDU website[3] to download puzzles with a virtual Breakout box and locks. I stumbled upon a Twitter Breakout EDU chat one night. I noticed they were discussing Digital Breakout EDU, which I had never heard of. It turned out that the chat moderator was one of the creators. He is now a member of my PLN.

PERSONAL LEARNING NETWORK: CULTURE

Writing for Publications

I never considered Library Media Tech Talk to be a publication, but indeed it is. When a person chooses to blog, it is an ongoing journey of the author's experiences. I also discovered that blogging allowed me to continue building a community by sharing my journey. It wasn't long before I was contacted by an editor of a new magazine called *School Library Connection*.[4] I had met this editor at a school library conference a few years before and had expressed a desire to write for journals. By having a blog, publishers can easily read a potential contributor's writing and content. I have read that anyone desiring to be published should begin with a blog. Having a school library blog surely helped me have an opportunity to write for *School Library Connection*. It also allowed me the opportunity to contribute to other blogs like SimpleK12[5] and Britannica Digital Learning.[6] As you can see, blogging and social media easily complement each other as important forms of establishing an online presence. In addition, I have connected with new friends in the library field when they reach out to me after reading one of my blog articles that resonates with them. This had led to Skype sessions and other collaborations.

Microsoft Innovative Educator Experts

Being involved in social media has allowed connections that have made a big difference in my own professional development. One of the most exciting organizations that I have had the opportunity to be a part of is the Microsoft Innovative Educator Expert (MIEExpert) group.[7] I learned about this organization through one of my PLN contacts. The MIEExpert group has the purpose of helping innovative educators around the world connect and grow using Microsoft products and interactions with each other. I have been able to regularly share about what collaborations we do in the library with MIEExpert membership and leadership through social media. Twitter, Facebook, and my blog have allowed my MIEExpert colleagues to have a window into my work at school. It has truly been life changing. This is because I have had direct interaction with Microsoft social media public relations via their Skype and Sway products. When I would tweet or write about our students using these tools, I would tag them in the post and they would respond to me nearly every time. Skype even sent me gifts (Skype T-shirt, lunch box, and other gear) that I shared with students. I was able to show them a benefit of having positive social media relations with a large company. This was a great way to model digital engagement.

There are other benefits that have changed me professionally as a result of being associated with MIEExperts. It is a global community of outstanding educators. Through the network, I have connected with many on social media. We have shared ideas and connected our students through Mystery Skype events. I was fortunate to be chosen by Microsoft to attend the MIEExpert Forum in Denver, Colorado, during the summer of 2016. Part of the criteria to be chosen as one of the one hundred educators to attend was that we had to be actively promoting our MIEExpert activities on social media. While at the forum, I was able to meet many of the friends I had connected with on social media on the Microsoft networks. It was a truly wonderful experience that I will discuss in depth later in the chapter. There were three other outstanding positives that came from being active in this group. One was that the MIEExpert leadership chose me to receive an award at the forum (for being active on social media and blogging in the community). The second was that they chose me to be a Microsoft Surface Expert in which they provided me a new Surface. The third was that I was selected to be a Skype Master Teacher. All of these experiences were a direct result of sharing relevant content on social media and growing my PLN. The impact has been increased connectivity with a growing educator network that pushes me to improve. This would not have occurred at this level without the "window" into my professional teaching practices that social media has provided to me. Even in the MIEExpert community, I have connected with numerous public school teacher librarians.

Characteristics of Community Building

Since becoming active on Twitter and other social media networks, I have noticed some common characteristics of connected educators that I regularly encounter. One of the most prevalent qualities I see is that connected educators and librarians have a growth mindset. These are commonly individuals that thrive on connecting with others and sharing ideas. They enjoy modeling exemplary practices for one another. I have noticed that connected educators are usually very positive people that seem to constantly post helpful artifacts on their social media outlets. They want to learn from others and they interact constantly.

Successful PLN participants are most frequently sharing blog posts, video clips, and media to reflect their learning. These actions constantly help others. PLN participants that are consistent at this tend to have the larger number of followers in their networks. My favorite people in my PLN are the ones that consistently respond when I send out messages with questions. They are also the ones that send encouraging responses to my informational posts. In a sense, they draw others in with their positive nature and professionalism.

It is fairly easy to find successful people to follow on social networks. One of the easiest ways to locate others is to look within specific hashtags related to one's profession. For me, hashtags related to school libraries and education have proven very beneficial to growing my PLN. Each of these hashtags also has a corresponding weekly, biweekly, or monthly chat. By monitoring these hashtags, one can see who the most active participants are. This is the method I have used for finding individuals to network with since I became active on Twitter. I have noticed anyone can be successful by incorporating the practices I have mentioned. In general, projecting professionalism, positive messages, helpful content, and encouraging others will draw others to you on social media.

Since becoming active on social media, I have been able to connect with thousands of educators around the country and world. While it is impossible to correspond regularly with that many educators, there are a few that have become friends through social media. To illustrate this, I would like to talk about several individuals who are public school librarians. Through Twitter and other electronic means, we regularly visit and collaborate. These individuals help to keep me informed of the latest trends in our profession. It is important to point out that these are colleagues I would have never met if not for social media. Building a strong PLN has helped me become a better educator through these interactions.

Who: Lynn Kleinmeyer (@THLibrariZen)

How We Connected

Lynn Kleinmeyer is a teacher librarian in Iowa. She works primarily with elementary ages in the Titan Hill School District. I first connected with Lynn on an education chat in the fall of 2015. We were corresponding about a possible collaboration to bring our learners together. It seems that we lost track of each other in our busy work schedules, and then we reconnected in the spring of 2016. I remember that Lynn asked me to consider using the free Voxer app to send voice messages to her. I had heard other educators talk about Voxer, but I wasn't familiar with it. I decided to download the app and discovered we could send voice mails easily back and forth to one another.

What I Learned

Lynn and I began a weekly practice of giving each other updates through Voxer. We talked about our programs, best practices, celebrations, and challenges. I began to look forward to hearing all about Lynn's experiences, and I couldn't wait to share about my world with her. We had a program that connected our schools together using Skype. In the sessions, one of our twelfth-grade students, Anna, read to Lynn's younger elementary learners. It was a wonderful experience for her students and Anna. In the days after the event, Lynn got to hear from Anna through my Voxer app. Both Lynn and I shared photos of the event on Twitter. It was a great way to show how libraries can connect learners through the magic of technology.

Key PLN Takeaway

There are leaders in our field waiting to join our PLN. When we connect, we can learn from each other.

Who: Elizabeth Hutchinson (@Elizabethutch)

How We Connected

I received a tweet from Elizabeth on a Saturday in January of 2016. She had read my blog post about our first Mystery Skype event, and she had messaged about how exciting it sounded. I quickly responded to her, thanking her for the encouraging words, and then I looked at her profile to see where she was located. Elizabeth is a librarian on the island of Guernsey, which is located in the English Channel. Elizabeth was able to help us have our first Mystery Hangout with one of the schools she serves on the island of Alderney. Elizabeth and I stayed in contact via Twitter over the following months. In February, Elizabeth spoke to our three other district librarians at my school via Google Hangouts for our regular professional development training meeting. She shared about her best practices and the impact that our recent Mystery Hangout had on the students at Alderney. It was a wonderful way to model the benefits of being connected educators to all that attended.

I was able to convince Elizabeth to connect with me on Voxer, and we started a practice of sharing weekly happenings. Elizabeth and I also connected via Skype a few times just to visit and talk about best practices as librarians. It has been a transformative international connection for me. I enjoyed our visits so much that I invited Elizabeth to connect with us during my summer 2016 breakout session at the Arkansas Association of School Librarians Conference held in Little Rock, Arkansas. The session was about using social media in the library, and I asked Elizabeth to connect via Skype and share about our Mystery Hangout sessions. Several Arkansas school librarians attended the session.

What I Learned

A growing PLN allows us to connect with nearly anyone in the world.

Key PLN Takeaway

Be willing to connect with new international colleagues.

Who: Tracey Wong (@TraceyCarayol)

How We Connected

Tracey Wong is an elementary public school librarian in New York. I first connected with Tracey after reading an article she had written in *Library Media Connection*. I e-mailed Tracey and told her how her article about library advocacy had resonated with me. After this we began e-mailing each other, and we eventually connected on Twitter, Facebook, and Voxer. Tracey encouraged me to apply for the Microsoft Innovative Educator Experts, and she was instrumental in my acceptance to the group. Tracey and I are currently planning to connect our students for collaborative library programming.

What I Learned

Tracey is a mentor I might have never met if I hadn't decided to reach out after reading her article. She changed my professional life by helping me get into the Microsoft Innovative Educator Expert community.

Key PLN Takeaway

Take risks and connect with those whom you admire professionally. They may join your PLN and help you grow in unforeseen ways.

Who: Karey Killian (@CoLIBRAtoRY)

How We Connected

Karey Killian is an elementary public school librarian in Pennsylvania. I connected with Karey on Twitter through the Microsoft Innovative Educator Expert network. Karey and I decided to connect our learners toward the end of spring in 2016. We had our eighth-grade learners give her fifth-grade students tips on Mystery Skype. It was a wonderful student-led event. We also connected our students again in the fall of 2016 and had our eighth-grade students read picture books to her first graders. Karey and I stay in touch via Twitter.

What I Learned

Karey is one of the most positive and uplifting school librarians I have met. Her positivity and professionalism greatly impact me. We should surround ourselves with people like this!

Key PLN Takeaway

Add people to your PLN who will build you up.

Deepening the Connection: Meeting My PLN

I had a great opportunity to attend the 2016 Microsoft Innovative Educator Expert Forum in Denver, Colorado. This was exciting on so many levels: learning with others in the group and actually meeting members of my PLN face-to-face. I was curious to see what it would be like to visit with these people in person. I quickly discovered that it was just like meeting old friends. I was able to meet Tracey Wong and Karey Killian at the forum. We talked to each other so easily. In fact, it was difficult to leave Denver after being around so many passionate educators for two days. Meeting in person seemed to strengthen our professional relationships.

My wife and I decided to stop by to meet Lynn Kleinmeyer and her family on the way home from Denver. Lynn actually lives in Nebraska and commutes to her job in Iowa. I was very excited to meet Lynn because I had interacted with her more than most of my other PLN members. Meeting Lynn was the same phenomenon I experienced in Denver; it was as if we had known each other for years. My wife and I got to spend a full day with Lynn and her family. We still stay in regular contact.

NEXT STEPS

Even as I write this, more exciting connections are being made. I hope to continue connecting and meeting more educator friends who will help me improve for my learning community. I aspire to connect with thought leaders in librarianship and learn from them. We should work to connect with people who will inspire us and challenge us. We should also model these connections for our learners so they might experience the resources available to them on social media.

I encourage you to take your device to begin networking and building a PLN using the methods I have shared. There is a very big world out there full of passionate and talented educators. When we surround ourselves with such colleagues, their practices will influence us. Social media is a network full of opportunities to connect and grow. I am truly excited to think about the future and what exciting connections await me in my practice of librarianship.

NOTES

1. "Tlchat," hashtag, Twitter, twitter.com/hashtag/tlchat.
2. Library Media Tech Talk (blog), librarymediatechtalk.blogspot.com/.
3. Digital Breakout EDU, www.breakoutedu.com/digital/.
4. School Library Connection, blog.schoollibraryconnection.com/.
5. SimpleK12, simplek12.com.
6. Britannica Digital Learning, britannicalearn.com.
7. For more information, see www.microsoft.com/en-us/education/educators/miee/default.aspx?Search=true.

III

TRANSFORMING COMMUNITY
INTO ACTION—SOCIAL MEDIA
AND SOCIAL JUSTICE

8

The Urgency and Agency of #OccupyNassau

Actively Archiving Anti-Racism at Princeton

Jarrett M. Drake

OVERVIEW

On August 9, 2014, as Michael Brown Jr.'s black and bruised body lay bare under a suburban St. Louis sun, a renewed resistance to anti-racism returned. The public display of his murdered body forever changed the lives of those Ferguson, Missouri, residents who saw it in person and it changed the lives of concerned citizens who watched events unfold over Twitter, primarily through the hashtag #BlackLivesMatter. Although the hashtag—and later an organization of the same name—originated from the labor of three black queer women from California's Bay Area, protesters in Ferguson adopted the hashtag to share vital information regarding the resistance and to counter narratives emerging through mainstream media about Brown and the protesters. The Ferguson resistance relied upon the labor of not only working-class citizens such as fast-food restaurant workers and pharmacy technicians but also relied upon a group central to previous struggles for civil and human rights: college students.

College students who flocked to Ferguson to fight for justice came back to their campuses ready to take the fight to their respective university administrations. The school year following Brown's murder saw a number of die-ins, sit-ins, and teach-ins to protest the accelerated assault on black bodies in American society, and it is within this context that students at Princeton University formed the Black Justice League (BJL) in November of 2014 to "[stand] in solidarity with Ferguson and [dismantle] racism on our campus."[1] That second goal, dismantling racism at Princeton, consisted of both public actions and private conversations with university administrators. One of its earliest public actions, a die-in outside the main student center, took shape on December 4, 2014, and responded to a New York City grand jury's decision not to indict police officer Daniel Pantaleo for his use of an illegal choke hold in the death of Eric Garner.[2] One of its earliest private conversations, a meeting of the Council of the Princeton University Community (CPUC), occurred less than one week after news of the decision not to indict officer Pantaleo. In that meeting, attended by the president, provost, dean of the college, and head of campus life, the BJL presented an open letter to the council that read in part:

> We are a group of Princeton University students who have united organically and in unanimous agreement that the recent public examples of police brutality and violations of black personhood are both unacceptable and inadmissible. . . . This national issue has illuminated campus problems of overt racism, microaggressions, stereotyping, and exclusion that we aim to transform. We have collectively identified our concerns related to current University policies that we believe implicitly promote a campus culture acceptant of racial animus and insensitivity. As such, in this document we outline a set of recommendations necessary to improve the experience for students of color on campus, specifically and facilitating a more accepting campus community at large.[3]

One of the letter's recommendations called for required diversity training for all staff and the transformation of certificate programs in ethnic studies into full academic departments. While one of the certificate programs, African American Studies, achieved department status later that academic year, the call for mandatory diversity trainings did not materialize. As such, the following academic school year, 2015–2016, began with issues unresolved from the previous one. In that year's time, the BJL connected with black students from other colleges to plan strategically how best to present anti-racism initiatives and ideas to their respective university administrations. From those connections, a collective of black college students, the Black Liberation Collective (BLC), organized a national day of action that ushered in a distinctly new wave of black student organizing: #StudentBlackOut.[4]

#StudentBlackOut galvanized the momentum sparked by the chiefly black women's organizing efforts at the University of Missouri under the banner #Concerned Student1950. The Missouri campaign led to the ouster of the university's president and chancellor as well as a national discourse on racism at American colleges. Taking its cue from Missouri and at the loose aegis of the BLC, on November 18, 2015, students at dozens of colleges in the United States and Canada staged walkouts and held demonstrations to present clear and compelling cases of institutional racism within the walls of their campus.[5] At Princeton, the BJL organized a sit-in at the university's main administrative building, Nassau Hall, to present a petition listing some of the demands it made a year earlier in the CPUC meeting.

Negotiations over the demands in that petition, which the BJL titled #Occu pyNassau, lasted two days and attracted international news coverage.[6] The petition posited three demands. First, it called for official university acknowledgment of the racist policies of former Princeton president and later U.S. president Woodrow Wilson as well as the removal of his name and image from several prominent campus landmarks. Second, it demanded cultural competency training for all faculty and staff members, echoing a previous plea. Third, the petition sought a space on

Figure 8.1. #OccupyNassau Petition, 2015, Black Justice League Records, Princeton University Archives, Department of Rare Books and Special Collections, Princeton University Library, wayback.archive-it.org/5151/20160109013534/https://www.change .org/p/princeton-university-administration-occupynassau-meet-black-student-s-demands

campus, cultural or otherwise, specifically for black students. Over the course of the thirty-two-hour sit-in, Princeton students and alumni shared thousands of social media posts with the hashtag #OccupyNassau expressing a range of reactions, from support and sanction to disagreement and disapproval.

It is not the purpose of this chapter to comment on the content of the #OccupyNassau petition. Its origins, stretching back to the murder of Michael Brown Jr., are provided here only to contextualize the genesis of the student group responsible for bringing forward the specific aims and avenues to address racism within the university. Rather, this chapter will narrate the considerations and choices that archivists at the Princeton University Archives made while documenting #OccupyNassau and will conclude by contextualizing this decision-making process within the concept of the active archive.

DOCUMENTING #OccupyNassau

Archivists at the Princeton University Archives began discussing how and whether to document #OccupyNassau within the first few hours of the sit-in. Much in the same way that the #OccupyNassau campaign followed the footsteps of freedom fighters in Ferguson, our approach to documenting #OccupyNassau was likewise informed by the archivists who worked proactively to preserve records of those same Ferguson freedom fighters. As if to foreshadow the next day's events, Temple University Libraries hosted the panel "Diversity in the Archives: Preserving Ephemeral Activist Culture" on November 17, 2015, the day before #StudentBlackOut and #OccupyNassau. A member of our team attended that panel, which featured three archivists—Dr. Meredith Evans, Bergis Jules, and Ed Summers—central to the project Documenting Ferguson and the separate but related project of collecting approximately thirteen million tweets of the #Ferguson hashtag.[7] We considered the wise words of the archivists who had already successfully documented "the now," leading us to pursue three pathways to document #OccupyNassau: (1) connect with colleagues, (2) consider the consequences, and (3) capture content and consent. These pathways were not pursued sequentially but contemporaneously and iteratively over the days and weeks following the protest.

Connect with Colleagues

The protest's urgency prompted our urgency. Normally, we at the University Archives convene a monthly digital curation meeting to discuss everything from potential acquisitions of born-digital archival collections to prospective changes in approaches for processing the collections once they arrive. These meetings, held on the second Thursday of each month, provide an essential space in which archivists communicate crucial information and coordinate efforts. The flow of our meeting schedule meant that we would not convene again until three weeks after the protest, so rather than allow almost a month and a major holiday to pass, a subset of the digital curation team convened a concise "huddle" on the morning following #OccupyNassau. The purpose of the huddle can be explained by further evoking the context of the analogy's origin: in football, a quarterback brings together teammates in a circle to discuss various options and to make a decision on which option best serves the end goal. Our huddle on the morning of November 19 was no different and proved just as effective.

Minutes before our scheduled huddle, I posed a question on Twitter to fellow archivists: "(How) is your university archives ethically, responsibly, and critically documenting #StudentBlackOut protests occurring right now?" The question's framing owes credit to the aforementioned archivists who documented the Ferguson resistance. Just four archivists responded with specific plans, stating their combined intentions to conduct oral history interviews, initiate consent-based web archiving, and host an open house for student activists to deposit their organization's archival records. But one of the responding archivists, Eira Tansey at the University of Cincinnati, engaged the question with me over a private Twitter conversation. Our chat blossomed into an idea to host a conference call that would be open to anyone interested in the original question of preserving records from these protests in critical, ethical, and responsible ways. The protests' urgency, again, dictated that we could not allow significant time to elapse before holding the call; hence, we scheduled it to take place the following day, November 20, and tweeted a link to a public Google Sheet that allowed anyone to state their intent to join us.

Close to three dozen archivists signed up for the call, representing institutional as well as geographical variety: black colleges in the South, private research universities on the coasts, and large public universities in the Midwest were among the many types of archival repositories present for the conversation. And because of that variety and volume of interest, Eira and I strongly recommended participants complete a homework assignment in advance so that the conversation would contain both substance and structure. Eira chose readings for the homework and I crafted discussion questions, the reactions to which we shared with the participants before the call.

Over a dozen archivists answered the questions before the call, and their responses reflected the range of institutions that participated. Many archivists expressed concerns for privacy as well as reticence about when and whether they should document #StudentBlackOut given that the issues students rose were (and are) very much unresolved. The failure of archives to foment trust with black student communities emerged as a consistent theme preventing the solicitation of non-public archival records such as meeting notes, organizational documents, or correspondence. Regarding the capture of social media pages administered by students, a considerable number of archivists retained a healthy dose of skepticism about the ethics of preserving these public sites without student consent or permission. Although one might expect that the volume and variety of the record keeping technologies used during #StudentBlackOut would concern archivists the most, the core conversation repeatedly returned to the right (or lack thereof) to aggregate massive amounts of

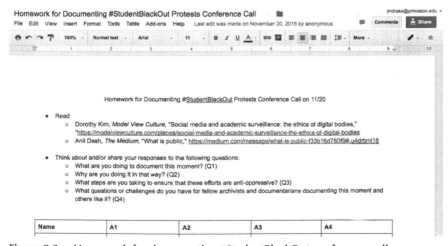

Figure 8.2.   Homework for documenting #StudentBlackOut conference call

social media data without consent, a testament to the selection of readings chosen by Eira as well as the investment in the archivists on the call to preempt and prompt difficult dialogue about the purpose, place, and position of a college archive.

Consider the Consequences

Our purpose as a college archive—at a liberal arts college, especially—commanded that we consider the full range of actions, inactions, and their respective consequences. An incident at the University of Missouri during the #Concerned Student1950 campaign illustrates this need vividly. Students who led the campaign as well as those demonstrating allyship to their cause sought to convene a space around a camp that emerged to support a graduate student, Jonathan Butler, who began a hunger strike to challenge the university system's racism and force their resignation of the system's president. Following the president's resignation on the morning of November 9, 2015, students formed a circle to rejoice about the victory, reflect on the struggle at large, and create a safe space. Tim Tai, a photojournalist and undergraduate student at the university who was on assignment for a national media outlet, demanded that the #ConcernedStudent1950 campaign allow him to photograph them and their activities. Tai justified the righteousness of his demand on the First Amendment, at which point one of the founders of the campaign and a fellow undergraduate student, Storm Ervin, intervened to respond to Tai's assertions and plead for his understanding:

> Ervin: Okay . . . please protect our space as human beings, okay?
>
> Tai: There's not a law around that.
>
> Ervin: Forget a law, how about humanity? Or respect?
>
> Tai: Well, how about documenting this for posterity?[8]

Tai's response, that documentation for posterity supersedes the humanity of black people, exemplifies one of several consequences that emerge when documentarians, be they archivists or journalists, prioritize their professional precepts over a people's plea for compassion. The legality of Tai's actions notwithstanding, the fervor of his demand demonstrates the danger of documentarians who fail to recognize that a *legal right* to be present in a space says nothing of a *moral duty* once inside said space. The encounter between Tai and Ervin raises two related possible consequences we considered before our documentation of #OccupyNassau: an expansion of surveillance and the cost of inaction.

To actively aggregate social media content produced by college students without their consent amplifies an already aggressive surveillance apparatus. Speech said in public does not equate to public speech. Moreover, speech said in public does not imply consent for the recording and distribution of that speech in perpetuity. In cases where a subset of the population is pursuing justice, it becomes even more incumbent that archivists adhere to those realities and recognize those risks.

A college archive that assumes an absolute authority—especially those with "good" intentions—to document these events may provide their institutions with an avenue through which to enact reprisals or retaliation against an already vulnerable group within a community. As seen with the state surveillance of protesters during the April 2015 Baltimore Uprising following the murder of Freddie Gray, the vast information captured in photographs, tweets, or other social media posts can offer authorities unprecedented powers to monitor and marginalize, making it the responsibility of the archivist to be aware of this possible if not likely usage.[9] As #OccupyNassau unfolded, archivists at Princeton were indeed aware of this usage and we weighed its prospects considerably before committing to a course of action.

Nevertheless, we weighed the possible expansion of surveillance against the cost of inaction. Consequences of inaction are less obvious than those of action but are no less severe. The essential question for us became: what might happen if the Princeton University Archives obtained no records of #OccupyNassau from the perspective of the students who penned the petition and organized the sit-in? (Un)fortunately, this question could move beyond a hypothetical one, as Lae'l Hughes-Watkins, university archivist at Kent State University, had already answered this question through her stewardship of Kent State's Black Campus Movement Project. When attempting to identify records at her repository documenting the Black Campus Movement at Kent State, Hughes-Watkins not only laments the paucity of information but also outlines a strategy aimed at addressing the gap.[10] A team member at Princeton consulted her article in the midst of #OccupyNassau, and it became clear that unlike the thousands of analog photographs collected retroactively from Kent State's Black Campus Movement Project, the born-digital photographs, iPhone videos, and other dynamic content shared via social media about #OccupyNassau would simply disappear into digital dust if the Princeton University Archives failed to take a moral but critical action to document the moment.

Capture Content and Consent

The moment's urgency left archivists with two choices for documenting #OccupyNassau that equally complicated consent. The first, a subject-based approach, would involve a strategy similar to the one Ed Summers and Bergis Jules deployed regarding #Ferguson: using a web crawler to capture every public tweet that mentioned #OccupyNassau. While this option may have captured a more representative real-time reaction to the protest, this path would have made obtaining consent difficult if not impossible, as doing so would have required archivists first to contact hundreds of individuals, some of whom likely were not members of the university community. For those within the community, a capture of this sort could wade into the gray area of the Family Educational Rights and Privacy Act (FERPA), the canary in the coal mine for college archivists. The second strategy, a provenance-based approach, would involve capturing the social media accounts of the organization responsible for the protest, the Black Justice League, as well as the accounts and websites of student news organizations providing live coverage of the event. After a successful capture of content, we would retain provisional copies of the content in such a fashion that the data could be destroyed if the organizations refused consent. While this strategy would exclude from the archival record the varied reactions to the days' events, it meant that archivists could obtain consent from a handful of records' creators as opposed to hundreds.

The second strategy emerged as the most critical, ethical, and responsible method for the University Archives to document #OccupyNassau. In addition to agreeing to capture content from the BJL's Twitter and Facebook pages, we identified two student news organizations—the *University Press Club* and the *Princeton Progressive*—that chronicled the events in real time by live-tweeting verbatim transcripts of dialogue between the students and administration. Using our recently purchased subscription to the Internet Archive's Archive-It service, we created two private seeds for each of the three organizations and ran test crawls of each seed beginning on Friday, November 20. We ran repeated test crawls on each seed for the next six days, as we surmised that the immediate sit-in would have subsided within that time. However, had it persisted, we planned to continue the capture process until its conclusion.

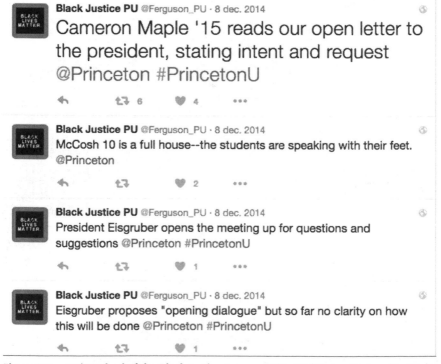

Figure 8.3. Twitter feed of the Black Justice League (BJL) at Princeton University, "Twitter Feed, 2014–2015, Black Justice League Records," Princeton University Archives, Department of Rare Books and Special Collections, Princeton University Library, wayback. archive-it.org/5151/20151124151000/https://twitter.com/Ferguson_PU/

Princeton Progresive @princetonprog · 18 nov.
BJL Student- "I don't understand why Wilson's name has to be on the building in order to acknowledge the things that he's done"

Princeton Progresive @princetonprog · 18 nov.
Eisgruber- "I agree that we have to be explicit and acknowledge the racism of Princeton"

Princeton Progresive @princetonprog · 18 nov.
Students currently occupying President Eisgruber's office in Nassau Hall

Figure 8.4. Twitter feed of the *Princeton Progressive*, "The Progressive Twitter Feed, 2015," Princeton University Publications Collection, Princeton University Archives, Department of Rare Books and Special Collections, Princeton University Library, wayback. archive-it.org/5151/20151124150958/https://twitter.com/princetonprog/

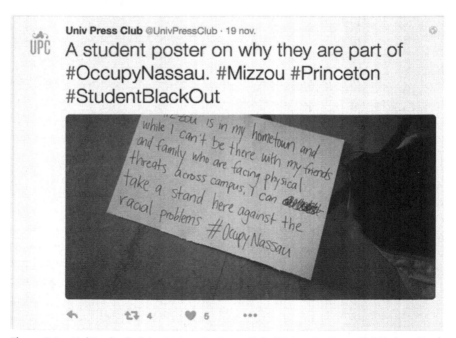

Univ Press Club @UnivPressClub · 19 nov.
A student poster on why they are part of #OccupyNassau. #Mizzou #Princeton #StudentBlackOut

Figure 8.5. Twitter feed of the *University Press Club*, "University Press Club Twitter Feed, 2009–2015," Princeton University Publications Collection, Princeton University Archives, Department of Rare Books and Special Collections, Princeton University Library, wayback .archive-it.org/5151/20151124151006/https://twitter.com/univpressclub

Because the Archive-It software allows archival repositories up to sixty days to determine whether it wants to retain test crawl data, the University Archives had a two-month window in which to obtain consent or destroy the content from the Archive-It account. As such, we withheld the urge to contact students during the protest or its immediate aftermath, instead choosing to contact them over e-mail close to a month later. Of the three student organizations contacted, two responded positively and one, a news group, did not respond altogether. Because the unresponsive group was a news organization, we retained its content anyway on the premise that a news entity's general purpose to publish and disseminate news gave tacit consent that its statements and contents were published in a public manner altogether different from individuals, students, and other types of organizations. If, for instance, a student political group did not *explicitly* consent to a capture of its social media and other web content, we would not capture it. This inaction, which again poses its own set of consequences, aligns with our affirmation of students' agency and respect for a group's right to determine the destruction or retention of its records.

The three pathways pursued at the Princeton University Archives—connect with colleagues, consider the consequences, and capture content and consent—evinced themselves to be equally essential to capture the more than one hundred thousand documents and six million kilobytes we collected through the documentation of #OccupyNassau. By tapping the expertise of professionals at other institutions, we put our fingers on the pulse of archival practice within the domain of social media archiving, as prior to #OccupyNassau we had not so much as attempted to capture data from Facebook or Twitter. Through evaluation of advantages and disadvantages of multiple options, we refrained from reinforcement of existing power dynamics and inequalities within our community. In the course of collecting content and seeking consent, we amassed a treasure trove of future historical documentation and did so in an explicitly unobtrusive and anti-oppressive manner. Our approach to documenting #OccupyNassau represents a method more than a model, and it is a method we have since honed and integrated into our practice for acquiring, preserving, and providing access to born-digital content of all genres.

Toward an Active Archive

To label, as some in the field of libraries and archives have, this method as "archival activism" or "activist archiving" undermines the power of those two concepts and obfuscates the quotidian realities of archival work within a corporation (such as a private university) or government body. Andrew Flinn, professor of archival studies at University College London, adds clarity to the obfuscation by defining those two concepts and two more related but distinct approaches: active archiving and archiving activism. The distinctions within the four concepts, like those in any classification scheme, form flexible boundaries, which Flinn acknowledges. Yet it is critical to note—especially for archivists embedded within larger institutions—that the method the Princeton University Archives used to document #OccupyNassau most directly aligns with active archiving, which Flinn defines as "an approach to archival practice which . . . acknowledges the role of the recordkeeper in 'actively' participating in the creation, management and pluralization of archives."[11]

Additionally, an active archive also entails recognition of the *facts* of structural inequalities and oppressions as well as the archive's and its parent institution's role in sustaining them. Silence and inaction, in the face of oppression, constitute speech and action. As such, it is incumbent on the active archivist not only to speak truth to power about structural inequalities but also to envision herself intervening *through* her capacity and duty as a professional, not in spite of it. The active archivist adheres to the aphorism of the librarian and poet Audre Lorde:

> In the transformation of silence into language and action, it is vitally necessary for each one of us to establish or examine her function in that transformation and to recognize her role as vital within that transformation.[12]

It follows that active archiving is not an option for institutional archivists but a responsibility and obligation to use one's archival might—through processes such as appraisal, arrangement, and description—to interrogate if not destabilize structures of oppression, not simply ignore them. An active archivist necessarily reimagines the role of the archive within a community, organization, or institution and part of that reimagination might lead our field to one that reduces inequality, not replicates it. Yet, as #OccupyNassau demonstrates, the urgency of the archivist to react must not subvert the agency of communities to resist. Respecting this resistance will be ever more necessary in the years ahead.

NOTES

1. "Facebook Page, 2014–2015, Black Justice League Records," Princeton University Archives, Department of Rare Books and Special Collections, Princeton University Library, wayback.archive-it.org/5151/20151128050615/http://www.facebook.com/BlackJusticeLea guePU/info/?ref=page_internal.

2. "No Indictment in Eric Garner Police Killing," *New York Amsterdam News*, December 3, 2014, amsterdamnews.com/news/2014/dec/03/no-indictment-eric-garner-police-killing/.

3. Minutes, 2011–2016, Council of the Princeton University Community Records, Princeton University Archives, Department of Rare Books and Special Collections, Princeton University Library, wayback.archive-it.org/5151/20160426191502/http://www.princeton .edu/vpsec/cpuc/Dec-12.pdf.

4. "StudentBlackOut," Black Liberation Collective, accessed December 15, 2016, www .blackliberationcollective.org/first-campaign/.

5. Jessica Glenza, "University Students Hold Anti-racism Protests across US," *Guardian*, November 18, 2015, www.theguardian.com/us-news/live/2015/nov/18/studentblackout-anti-racism-protests-universities.

6. "Princeton Considers Dropping Woodrow Wilson Name after Protests," *BBC*, November 20, 2015, www.bbc.com/news/world-us-canada-34883289.

7. "Continuing Education Committee—Diversity in the Archives: Preserving Ephemeral Activist Culture," Academic Assembly of Librarians (Temple University Libraries), November 17, 2015, sites.temple.edu/academicassembly/2015/11/17/continuing-education-committee-2/.

8. Caitlin Campbell, "Protesters' Confrontations with Journalists Spark First Amendment Debate," *Columbia Daily Tribune*, November 10, 2015, www.columbiatribune.com/news/local/protesters-confrontations-with-journalists-spark-first-amendment-debate/article_074e28b7-542c-5862-bb07-cc5bfb689086.html.

9. Matthew Cagle, "Facebook, Instagram, and Twitter Provided Data Access for a Surveillance Product Marketed to Target Activists of Color," American Civil Liberties Union, October 11, 2016, www.aclu.org/blog/free-future/facebook-instagram-and-twitter-provided-data-access-surveillance-product-marketed.

10. Lae'l Hughes-Watkins, "Filling in the Gaps: Using Outreach Efforts to Acquire Documentation on the Black Campus Movement, 1965–1972," *Archival Issues* 36, no. 1 (2014): 27–42, minds.wisconsin.edu/handle/1793/73931.

11. Andrew Flinn, "'Humanizing an Inevitably Political Craft': Introduction to the Special Issue on Archiving Activism and Activist Archiving," *Archival Science* 15, no. 4 (2015): 331.

12. Audre Lorde, "The Transformation of Silence into Language and Action," in *I Am Your Sister: Collected and Unpublished Writings of Audre Lorde*, ed. Rudolph P. Byrd, Johnnetta Betsch Cole, and Beverly Guy-Sheftall (Oxford: Oxford University Press, 2009), 42.

BIBLIOGRAPHY

Cagle, Matthew. "Facebook, Instagram, and Twitter Provided Data Access for a Surveillance Product Marketed to Target Activists of Color." American Civil Liberties Union. October 11, 2016. www.aclu.org/blog/free-future/facebook-instagram-and-twitter-provided-data-access-surveillance-product-marketed.

Campbell, Caitlin. "Protesters' Confrontations with Journalists Spark First Amendment Debate." *Columbia Daily Tribune*. November 10, 2015. www.columbiatribune.com/news/local/protesters-confrontations-with-journalists-spark-first-amendment-debate/article_074e28b7-542c-5862-bb07-cc5bfb689086.html.

"Continuing Education Committee—Diversity in the Archives: Preserving Ephemeral Activist Culture." Academic Assembly of Librarians (Temple University Libraries). November 17, 2015. sites.temple.edu/academicassembly/2015/11/17/continuing-education-committee-2/.

"Facebook Page, 2014–2015, Black Justice League Records." Princeton University Archives, Department of Rare Books and Special Collections, Princeton University Library. wayback.archive-it.org/5151/20151128050615/http://www.facebook.com/BlackJusticeLeaguePU/info/?ref=page_internal.

Flinn, Andrew. "'Humanizing an Inevitably Political Craft': Introduction to the Special Issue on Archiving Activism and Activist Archiving." *Archival Science* 15, no. 4 (2015): 329–335.

Glenza, Jessica. "University Students Hold Anti-racism Protests across US." *Guardian*. November 18, 2015. www.theguardian.com/us-news/live/2015/nov/18/studentblackout-anti-racism-protests-universities.

Hughes-Watkins, Lae'l. "Filling in the Gaps: Using Outreach Efforts to Acquire Documentation on the Black Campus Movement, 1965–1972." *Archival Issues* 36, no. 1 (2014): 27–42. minds.wisconsin.edu/handle/1793/73931.

Lorde, Audre. "The Transformation of Silence into Language and Action." In *I Am Your Sister: Collected and Unpublished Writings of Audre Lorde*. Edited by Rudolph P. Byrd, Johnnetta Betsch Cole, and Beverly Guy-Sheftall. Oxford: Oxford University Press, 2009, 39–43.

Minutes, 2011–2016, Council of the Princeton University Community Records, Princeton University Archives, Department of Rare Books and Special Collections, Princeton University Library. wayback.archive-it.org/5151/20160426191502/http://www.princeton.edu/vpsec/cpuc/Dec-12.pdf.

"No Indictment in Eric Garner Police Killing." *New York Amsterdam News*. December 3, 2014. amsterdamnews.com/news/2014/dec/03/no-indictment-eric-garner-police-killing/.

#OccupyNassau Petition, 2015, Black Justice League Records, Princeton University Archives, Department of Rare Books and Special Collections, Princeton University Library. wayback.archive-it.org/5151/20160109013534/https://www.change.org/p/princeton-university-administration-occupynassau-meet-black-student-s-demands.

"Princeton Considers Dropping Woodrow Wilson Name after Protests." *BBC*. November 20, 2015. www.bbc.com/news/world-us-canada-34883289.

"StudentBlackOut." Black Liberation Collective. Accessed December 15, 2016. www.blackliberationcollective.org/first-campaign/.

9

Cultivating Critical Dialogue on Twitter

April M. Hathcock

SOCIAL RESPONSIBILITY AND
SOCIAL MEDIA IN LIBRARIANSHIP

"Librarianship is not a neutral profession, and libraries are not neutral spaces."[1] For many librarians,[2] like the librarian founders of Storytime Underground, this statement could not be more true or more central to their daily working practice: managing information, educating the public about information literacy, developing systems, curating collections. For librarians who subscribe to critical consciousness—that is, those librarians concerned with issues of power, privilege, oppression, and social justice—all of this work is rooted in and affected by the events and circumstances happening in the world around them. Information institutions, like libraries and archives, are not neutral spaces because the world in which they exist are not neutral spaces. Moreover, it is the information professional's responsibility, as a curator of knowledge, to question and trouble these spaces from the inside out, as Chris Bourg, director of libraries at MIT, describes in her framework for bringing social justice into library work.[3] For the critically conscious information worker, there is no question about the non-neutrality of our work or the importance of bringing critical theory and practice, critical *praxis*, into our day-to-day duties. In fact, social responsibility and a commitment to diversity are built into our professional values.[4] As LIS educators, Sarah T. Roberts and Safiya Umoja Noble note, "Within the context of *professionalism* and *the field*, a socially responsible perspective mandates that students and scholars think about the ways in which deep entrenchments to narratives of neutrality, objectivity, and in many cases silence on social issues by LIS researchers and professionals have consequences."[5]

Thus, to be a critically conscious librarian is to understand the inherent importance of critical dialogue on weighty social issues such as race, gender, sexual orientation, gender identity, class, indigeneity, disability, religious freedom, and more.

Interestingly enough, however, some of the most productive and enriching of these conversations for critical librarians have been and are taking place on a social media platform that limits commentary to 140 characters or less. For many librarians seeking to engage with and learn from each other and their communities on these vital societal issues, Twitter has become a go-to digital space for initiating critical conversations, learning, listening, and growing.

Twitter is a public, web-based social media platform that allows participants to post 140-character microblogs or *tweets* onto their accounts to be shared openly on the web, or privately among their followers in the case of closed accounts. Twitter users can follow each other's accounts (denoted by the user names known as *handles*) to keep updated on tweets of people or institutions they know or care about. Likewise, Twitter also provides online spaces for public conversations on a variety of topics through the use of *hashtags*, a tagging system that allows Twitter users to participate in and the general public to follow along with topical tweets, such as #Indigenous PeoplesDay as an alternative to Columbus Day[6] or #Election2016 dealing with that year's devastating presidential election.[7]

Libraries and librarians have been early adopters of social media platforms such as Twitter for conducting outreach to library patrons and marketing library events. Just as important to this use of social media, however, has been the ways in which librarians use Twitter and other social media outlets for engaging in low-cost professional development.[8] Librarians use Twitter to explore subject area expertise related to their informational duties or as a networking tool to meet and interact with other professionals.[9] Finally, by combining the outreach and professional development capacity of social media, many librarians have even taken to using Twitter and like tools as a means of building community, both within the profession as well as among our larger communities. This community-building function of Twitter has been of particular value to critically conscious librarians looking for ways to derive "real-world social value from shared trust and shared vision"[10] by engaging in critical *micro-dialogues* with like-minded individuals. Twitter allows critical librarians to engage more deeply with social justice values and activism through connection with each other and with our broader communities.

CONNECTING WITH EACH OTHER:
#critlib AND #libleadgender

In so many ways, Twitter is invaluable for critical librarians to connect with each other across institutions, job titles, and geographic distances. For many librarians, engaging in critical work can feel like a solitary experience, so the benefit of joining with other like-minded librarians, even if it is only through 140-character microchats, can make a huge difference in motivation, learning, and professional growth. There are many ways in which critical librarians connect with each other via Twitter, from formal chats to informal information sharing on hashtags to more organic person-to-person connections.

One of the more organized connection points that has existed since 2014 is the #critlib hashtag and its accompanying chats (see figure 9.1).[11] #Critlib provides a space on Twitter for critical librarians to discuss a variety of issues central to their praxis: "Critlib is short for 'critical librarianship,' a movement of library workers dedicated to bringing social justice principles into our work in libraries. We aim to engage in discussion about critical perspectives on library practice. Recognizing that we all work under regimes of white supremacy, capitalism, and a range of structural inequalities, how can our work as librarians intervene in and disrupt those systems?"[12] In light of this mission, formally organized chats take place on a regular basis about twice a month on a topic chosen and moderated by librarians

Figure 9.1. Screenshots of tweets by Jessica Schomberg and Violet Fox from #critlib chat on supporting library workers with disabilities, Jessica Schomberg, Twitter post, December 6, 2016, twitter.com/schomj/status/806328902641709056; Violet Fox, Twitter post, December 6, 2016, twitter.com/violetbfox/status/806329606383038464

from around the world, though primarily from North America. Topics include a wide assortment of social justice issues relating to librarianship from building more inclusive public service points, to providing services to the homeless, to dealing with microaggressions in the profession.

The #critlib community has grown so much that it also sponsors physical, in-person gatherings for critical librarians. The first #critlib unconference took place in 2015 right before the Association of College and Research Libraries meeting in Portland, Oregon.[13] There have been other #critlib unconferences and meet-ups since then for those librarians able to travel to the meeting locations. Nonetheless, by far, the use of the Twitter hashtag has been crucial for librarians looking to connect with their colleagues elsewhere without the burden of travel costs. #Critlib provides a place for librarians interested in social justice praxis to learn from the experiences of others and feel even more connected to the profession: "The #critlib community and artifacts they create (conferences, website, etc.) have been really helpful. . . . It's

 **Amanda Meeks**
@A_meeksie

 👤⁺ Follow

Q2 How do you recognize, respect, & validate intersectional identities that surround you, whether they are visible or not? #libleadgender

5:12 PM - 14 Dec 2016

 **Krista Mccracken**
@kristamccracken

 👤⁺ Follow

Q2. Make space for intersectional and marganalized voices. Listen....a lot. Use my privilege to speak up #libleadgender

RETWEETS   LIKES
4   6

5:17 PM - 14 Dec 2016

Figure 9.2. Screenshots of tweets by Amanda Meeks and Krista Mccracken from #libleadgender chat on intersectional identities and privilege, Amanda Meeks, Twitter post, December 14, 2016, twitter.com/A_meeksie/status/809204450053062656; Krista Mccracken, Twitter post, December 14, 2016, twitter.com/kristamccracken/ status/809205692968161280

also really nice to know there are people out there thinking and excited about the same things as me."[14]

Another great organized space for critical dialogue among librarians on Twitter is the hashtag #libleadgender.[15] Started by library leaders Jessica Olin and Michelle Millet as an outgrowth of their article on gendered expectations of library leaders, the #libleadgender community is a space for periodic discussions and information sharing among librarians regarding issues related to gender and leadership.[16] Previous discussion topics have included strategies for maintaining self-care and methods for building more inclusive work spaces (see figure 9.2).[17] In a highly feminized profession,[18] having space to discuss the ways in which gender performativity and gender normativity affect our work as librarians can be vital to success in our day-to-day work.

Online communities for critical dialogue, such as #critlib and #libleadgender, are immensely useful to librarians who participate, but these communities also provide ample space for self-reflection and critique that includes the voices of those who do not participate. Two key elements of critical praxis are self-reflection and iterative critique; these elements are just as present in the micro-dialogue space of Twitter. For example, there has been at least one #critlib chat focused entirely on "critiquing #critlib," during which librarians who self-identify with the community and those who do not reflected on the ways the community fails to live up to its mission of inclusive dialogue on social justice.[19] Another #critlib chat titled "#feelings" encouraged participants to share reflections under the joint hashtag #whyicritlib.[20] While many included very positive stories about how the #critlib community has enriched their practice, there were also several others who included critical views of the ways the community has fallen short. The point is that, regardless of whether a librarian self-identifies with the Twitter community, the open dialogue space allows for everyone to share their reflections, good or bad, on what the community is and what it should be.

Aside from these more formal ways in which critical librarians connect via Twitter, using the #critlib, #libleadgender, and other hashtags, Twitter allows for other more organic means of connection between and among librarians interested in social justice. Because it is open to all types of users and accessible in countries all over the world, Twitter provides an opportunity for critically conscious librarians to connect across institutions and borders in ways that may never be possible in a physical space. Having this space to connect with others who share an interest in social justice can be invaluable for those of us who may feel isolated within our neoliberal institutions. It can be extremely isolating to feel like the only librarian struggling for justice and equity in an institution continuously focused on staying within constantly restrained budgets, meeting newer and higher assessment goals, or counting and valuing every task and encounter. However, with the online connections Twitter affords, socially conscious librarians can step out of the neoliberal, market- and business-driven spiral of their institutions and slow down to think, share, and engage in self-care with like-minded others all over the globe.[21]

Opportunities for organic connection are also vital to librarians for whom critical social justice is more than an interest but a way of life. For librarians from marginalized communities and identities, being able to connect with other librarians living their reality can make the difference between succeeding in the profession and leaving it altogether.[22] Critical conversations and connections that take place on Twitter provide a safer haven for navigating the profession from the margins. Particularly for new librarians of color, Twitter can be a natural fit for these connections: for example, research shows that 40 percent of Black Internet users between the ages of 18 and 29 use Twitter.[23] In a profession that is 88 percent White,[24] librarians of color, as well as librarians from other intersections of marginalized identity, need "access to a supportive group of similarly diverse-minded colleagues to whom they can relate and confide."[25]

As a librarian of color, I have myself benefited from and witnessed others benefiting from the organic connections for critical dialogue that Twitter affords. I have a number of colleagues from marginalized identities with whom I check in and connect on a regular basis and whom I may never have met if it were not for Twitter. We share stories of frustration and triumph; we teach and learn from one another; we encourage each other, all with the goal of staying true to our commitment to bring social justice praxis to our day-to-day library work. These connections have been absolutely essential to our continued success in the field. As librarians Tarida Anantachai, Latrice Booker, Althea Lazzaro, and Martha Parker note, "Professionals are generally better equipped to grow and succeed when they have such collegial group environments and networks at their disposal."[26]

Regardless of identity, though, Twitter provides a great place for librarians to connect with each other to engage in critical dialogue and broaden our social justice work. Critical dialogue on Twitter provides a space for listening, learning, and growth. It is a place for simultaneously learning from others and sharing our own experiences (figure 9.3). Engaging in these critical micro-conversations with like-minded professionals allows us to deepen our engagement with critical issues both within our libraries and beyond within our broader communities.

 **Erin Leach**
@erinaleach

 ⬩ Follow

I appreciate my Twitter community for teaching me how to talk about diversity and inclusion in a thoughtful and fearless way.

RETWEET LIKES
1   8

7:46 AM - 9 Sep 2016

Figure 9.3. Screenshot of tweet by Erin Leach (@erinaleach), Erin Leach, Twitter post, September 9, 2016, twitter.com/erinaleach/status/774257721596051457

CONNECTING WITH OUR COMMUNITIES

In addition to allowing critical librarians to connect with each other, Twitter also provides space for us to connect with the social justice issues of importance to our broader communities. Critical librarians recognize that our work does not occur in a vacuum, and we look to engage with the broader social justice issues of our time both within and without our library settings. For many of us, connecting with community advocacy and activism through Twitter provides an opportunity to connect personal and professional concerns and identities.

The use of Twitter to promote social justice advocacy is nothing new.[27] From the tweets arising out of the Arab spring protests of 2010; to the development of the #BlackLivesMatter hashtag and movement in 2012 by Alicia Garza, Patrisse Cullors, and Opal Tometi, three queer and queer-allied Black women enraged by the acquittal of the White man who killed Trayvon Martin, an unarmed Black teenager[28]; to the #noDAPL hashtag tracking protests against the forcible taking and contamination of Native lands for the building of the Dakota Access Pipeline,[29] Twitter has long been a valuable tool in galvanizing support for social justice movements around the world. For many advocacy groups, Twitter provides the key to "civic engagement and collective action," allowing people from vastly disparate backgrounds and physical locations to collect on a particular issue.[30]

It is no wonder that Twitter has proven to be such an integral element of widespread social justice movements. Since 2010, its user numbers have risen exponentially, from about thirty million monthly tweeters to more than three hundred million in late 2016.[31] Twitter connects even more people than it ever has before, making it a natural tool for spreading awareness and galvanizing action around social justice issues. What this means for critical librarians is that it makes for a natural social media platform for connecting beyond our own critical conversations to the discussions happening in our communities and the communities of others. The broad reach of Twitter allows critical librarians to integrate our "offline versus online" experiences,[32] such that our critical lives *on* social media can support and reflect our critical lives *off* social media.

This integration of online and offline social justice involvement has resulted in critical librarians connecting via Twitter with movements like #noDAPL, #Black LivesMatter, #TransLivesMatter,[33] and many others. While there are any number of librarians connecting with these movements on an individual basis, perhaps what is most noteworthy are the ways in which librarians are engaging in these movements collectively. For example, the Twitter account for #Libraries4Black-Lives[34] (@Libs4BlackLives) represents one such collective form of engagement.

Founded in the summer of 2016 by four public librarians from across the United States, #Libraries4BlackLives is a "call to action" for libraries and librarians to openly and proactively commit to the #BlackLivesMatter movement: "#BlackLivesMatter is an invitation to listen to the lived experiences of Black communities, to join in dismantling racism, and to affirm that 'embracing and defending Black life in particular has the potential to lift us all' (Alicia Garza, #BLM co-founder, July 2013)."[35] To that end, librarians Amita Lonial, Amy Sonnie, Jessica Anne Bratt, and Sarah Lawton developed a site to connect critical librarians directly to the Movement 4 Black Lives platform and actively encourage fellow professionals to join the more than forty thousand (as of late 2016) people who have signed the #M4BLpledge and affirmed their commitment to advocating for social justice in the lives of Black people. The #Libraries4BlackLives site also includes a number of resources for critical librarians to engage better with the movement not only in and through their libraries but with the broader Black and allied community (figure 9.4).[36]

While the #Libraries4BlackLives movement maintains a static web presence, its most effective and active means of connecting librarians and libraries with the activist community is via its Twitter account. Using the @Libs4BlackLives handle, Lonial, Sonnie, Bratt, and Lawton update library and non-library followers alike on news, actions, and events related to #BlackLivesMatter happening around the country. They also organize opportunities for critical librarians and the broader activist community to connect through tweet chats, call-ins, and conference meetups. The #Libraries4BlackLives team takes advantage of the broad reach of Twitter to engage librarians and the broader public in essential conversations about race, racism, and anti-racism. As Sonnie explained in a *Library Journal* interview,

> I believe deeply in learning from history, the civil rights movement and even further back . . . engaging new ideas, lifting up hidden and marginalized voices, and amplifying calls for a more free, democratic, and participatory future. . . . That is why I became a librarian. That is what I think this movement is calling on us to do now, to encourage people to explore these ideas and our interconnections, to provide information and provide space for people who are most impacted by racial injustice.[37]

Libraries4BlackLives
@Libs4BlackLives   👤 Follow

How is your library advancing discussion on race & racial justice? Share your work with #Libraries4BlackLives padlet.com/grpl/libraries...

RETWEETS   LIKES
12   15

12:59 PM - 8 Aug 2016

Figure 9.4.   Screenshot of tweet by #Libraries4BlackLives (@Libs4BlackLives), Libraries 4 Black Lives, Twitter post, August 8, 2016, twitter.com/Libs4BlackLives/status/7627400279 39880960

Another example of critical librarians collectively engaging with the community in critical dialogue is through the hashtag #librariesrespond.[38] The American Library Association's (ALA) Office for Diversity, Literacy, and Outreach Services started the hashtag during the summer of 2016 following the rash of hate-fueled killings in Orlando, Florida; Baton Rouge, Louisiana; Dallas, Texas; and many other locations across the United States.[39] Librarians and libraries were encouraged to share the ways they were supporting and advocating for their communities in the wake of these tragedies by posting pictures and messages under the #libraries respond tag. Critical librarians from across the country took up the challenge by sharing ways they were engaging their communities in critical dialogue on issues of racial profiling, police brutality, homophobia and transphobia, and other instances of hate and violence against marginalized groups. Postings included information about a library-run counseling hotline for community members affected by violence, #BlackLivesMatter book displays, and the provision of additional library hours and spaces for community members to gather and feel safe.[40] The librarians and libraries that participated in #librariesrespond used Twitter to draw attention to the work they were doing as part of their commitment to promoting social justice within their communities.

In a similar vein, the creation and use of the #LIUlockout hashtag[41] in the fall of 2016 helped to galvanize critical librarians worldwide around a labor cause affecting a number of university educators, including a number of academic librarians. At the start of the 2016–2017 academic year, administrators at Long Island University, Brooklyn (LIU), rather than continue to engage in contract negotiations, locked out unionized faculty for nearly two weeks.[42] Faculty had less than two days' notice before losing their benefits and pay, and students were left to begin the school year with unqualified administrators and other "scabs" filling in to teach their courses.[43] Using the hashtag #LIUlockout, LIU librarians, led in large part by Emily Drabinski, instruction coordinator for the library and union secretary, took to Twitter to spread awareness about what was happening in their campus community and to garner support. Thanks to the broad reach of Twitter, that support came in droves as fellow librarians, educators, and labor organizers rushed to send in letters of support, donate funds to help provide for the locked-out faculty and their families, and otherwise spread the word about the lockout. The Twitter outreach also inspired a #critlib chat on the #LIUlockout, during which critical librarians discussed ways to get involved in supporting the LIU community and labor movements in general.[44]

Finally, librarians also engage in critical community conversations on Twitter through involvement with the #WeNeedDiverseBooks[45] campaign, which began in 2014 through the efforts of authors Ellen Oh, Malinda Lo, Aisha Saeed, and others.[46] #WeNeedDiverseBooks is "a grassroots organization of children's book lovers that advocates essential changes in the publishing industry to produce and promote literature that reflects and honors the lives of all young people."[47] With the involvement of librarians, publishers, teachers, caretakers, and other community stakeholders, the #WeNeedDiverseBooks movement promotes the importance of published stories that include and even center characters beyond the traditional white, cisgender, heterosexual male. #WeNeedDiverseBooks is about advocating for the publication of more diverse books that reflect the realities of children of all races, ethnicities, sexual orientations, disabilities, religions, gender identities, and more. Using the hashtag, people from a broad range of backgrounds share their stories of how and why diverse books help those from otherwise marginalized identities find a sense of place and self by seeing themselves reflected in the characters they read. Likewise, with the #ownvoices hashtag,[48] developed by author Corinne Duyvis in 2015, critical librarians and other community members advocate for the publication of books about characters from marginalized identities that are written by authors from marginalized identities in their *own voices*.[49] Together, the #WeNeedDiverseBooks and #ownvoices hashtags provide an online space for critical librarians to engage in critical discussions surrounding publishing practices and the need for more diversity in children's, and other, literature.

FROM CONVERSATION TO ACTION

Thus, through hashtags like #Libraries4BlackLives, #librariesrespond, and #We NeedDiverseBooks, critical librarians engage with their communities in vital conversations about social justice issues that extend far beyond the immediate library context. However, these conversations merely represent the greater social justice work critical librarians are doing. The critical dialogues provide a much-needed place for planning, learning, and strategizing for the actual labor of advocacy and activism that highlight the day-to-day work and lives of librarians concerned with social justice issues. We engage in dialogue among ourselves and with our communities in order to inform our active work, which in turn provides additional topics for discussion in an iterative process of linking theory and practice into praxis.[50] It is through cultivating critical dialogue in online spaces like Twitter that we are better able to engage in critical action to improve the lives of our library users and our broader communities.

NOTES

1. Cory Eckert, "Opinion: Libraries Are Not Neutral," *School Library Journal*, August 2016, www.slj.com/2016/08/opinion/libraries-are-not-neutral-opinion/.
2. Throughout this chapter, I will refer to "librarians" and "librarianship," but for me, those terms encompass more than people with formal degrees in library and information science. I use those terms to refer to all library workers regardless of education, job title, or rank.
3. Chris Bourg, "Libraries, Technology, and Social Justice," The Feral Librarian (blog), October 7, 2016, chrisbourg.wordpress.com/2016/10/07/libraries-technology-and-social -justice/.

4. American Library Association, "Core Values of Librarianship," accessed November 21, 2016, www.ala.org/advocacy/intfreedom/statementspols/corevalues.

5. Sarah T. Roberts and Safiya Umoja Noble, "Empowered to Name, Inspired to Act: Social Responsibility and Diversity as Calls to Action in the LIS Context," *Library Trends* 64, no. 3 (2016): 515.

6. "Indigenouspeoplesday" hashtag, Twitter, twitter.com/hashtag/indigenouspeoplesday.

7. "Election2016" hashtag, Twitter, twitter.com/hashtag/election2016.

8. See chapters 6 and 7 in this book for more about personal learning networks.

9. Ernie J. Cox, "Twitter for All: Expanding Professional Dialogue with Social Media," *Library Media Connection* 28, no. 5 (2010): 52–53; Brian K. Kooy, "Building Virtually Free Subject Area Expertise through Social Media: An Exploratory Study," *College & Research Libraries* 77, no. 4 (2016): 423–54.

10. Scott W. H. Young and Doralyn Rossmann, "Building Library Community through Social Media," *Information Technology and Libraries* 34, no. 1 (2015): 21; Maria R. Lee, David C. Yen, and C. Y. Hsiao, "Understanding the Perceived Community Value of Facebook Users," *Computers in Human Behavior* 35 (June 2014): 355–56.

11. "Critlib" hashtag, Twitter, twitter.com/hashtag/critlib; Critlib.org, "About/Join the Discussion," accessed November 21, 2016, critlib.org/about/.

12. Critlib.org, "About."

13. Critlib Unconference 2015, "About," accessed November 21, 2016, critlib2015.wee bly.com/.

14. Eamon Tewell, "Putting Critical Information Literacy into Context: How and Why Librarians Adopt Critical Practices in Their Teaching," In the Library with the Lead Pipe, October 2016, www.inthelibrarywiththeleadpipe.org/2016/putting-critical-information-literacy -into-context-how-and-why-librarians-adopt-critical-practices-in-their-teaching/.

15. "Libleadgender" hashtag, Twitter, twitter.com/hashtag/libleadgender.

16. Jessica Olin and Michelle Millet, "Gendered Expectations for Leadership in Libraries," In the Library with the Lead Pipe, November 2015, www.inthelibrarywiththeleadpipe .org/2015/libleadgender/.

17. Jessica Olin, "#libleadgender and Self-Care," Storify (chat), October 5, 2016, storify. com/olinj/libleadgender-and-self-care; April M. Hathcock, "DO THE WORK!!! #liblead gender Chat March 9," At the Intersection (blog), March 4, 2016, aprilhathcock.wordpress .com/2016/03/04/do-the-work-libleadgender-chat-march-9/.

18. Olin and Millet, "Gendered Expectations."

19. Critlib.org, "Critiquing #critlib," accessed November 21, 2016, critlib.org/critiquing -critlib/.

20. Critlib.org, "Feelings," accessed November 21, 2016, critlib.org/feelings/.

21. Alison Mountz et al., "For Slow Scholarship: A Feminist Politics of Resistance through Collective Action in the Neoliberal University," *ACME: An International E-Journal for Critical Geographies* 14, no. 4 (2015): 1239.

22. Tarida Anantachai, Latrice Booker, Althea Lazzaro, and Martha Parker, "Establishing a Communal Network for Professional Advancement among Librarians of Color," in *Where Are All the Librarians of Color?*, ed. Rebecca Hankins and Miguel Juárez (Sacramento: Library Juice Press, 2015), 32–33; Emily K. Chan, Jovanni Lota, Holly A. Smith, and Steven D. Booth, "Discovering Librarianship: Personalizing the Recruitment Process for Under-Represented Students," in *Where Are All the Librarians of Color?*, ed. Rebecca Hankins and Miguel Juárez (Sacramento: Library Juice Press, 2015), 24.

23. Bergis Jules, "Documenting the Now Project," presentation, Collections as Data: Stewardship and Use Models to Enhance Access, Library of Congress, Washington, D.C., September 27, 2016.

24. American Library Association, "Diversity Counts 2009–2010 Update," accessed April 25, 2016, www.ala.org/offices/diversity/diversitycounts/2009-2010update.

25. Anantachai et al., "Establishing a Communal Network," 32.

26. Ibid.

27. Ann Dutton Ewbanks, "Library Advocacy through Twitter: A Social Media Analysis of #savelibraries and #getESEAright," *School Libraries Worldwide* 21, no. 2 (2015): 28.

28. "Blacklivesmatter" hashtag, Twitter, twitter.com/hashtag/blacklivesmatter; Wikipedia, s.v. "Black Lives Matter," last modified November 21, 2016, en.wikipedia.org/wiki/Black_Lives_Matter.

29. "Nodapl" hashtag, Twitter, twitter.com/hashtag/nodapl; The FANG Collective, #NoDAPL Solidarity (blog), accessed November 21, 2016, nodaplsolidarity.org/.

30. Dutton Ewbanks, "Library Advocacy," 28.

31. Ibid., 27; Statista, "Number of Monthly Active Twitter Users Worldwide from 1st Quarter 2010 to 3rd Quarter 2016 (in Millions)," accessed November 21, 2016, www.statista.com/statistics/282087/number-of-monthly-active-twitter-users/.

32. Young and Rossmann, "Building Library Community," 22; Jessica McLean, Sophia Maalsen, and Alana Grech, "Learning about Feminism in Digital Spaces: Online Methodologies and Participatory Mapping," *Australian Geographer* 47, no. 2 (2016): 160–61.

33. "Translivesmatter" hashtag, Twitter, twitter.com/hashtag/translivesmatter.

34. "Libraries4blacklives" hashtag, Twitter, twitter.com/hashtag/libraries4blacklives.

35. Libraries 4 Black Lives, "Take the Pledge," accessed November 21, 2016, libraries4blacklives.org/pledge/.

36. Libraries 4 Black Lives, "Your Ideas," accessed November 21, 2016, libraries4blacklives.org/yourideas/.

37. Lisa Peet, "Public Librarians Launch Libraries4BlackLives," *Library Journal*, August 2016, lj.libraryjournal.com/2016/08/people/public-librarians-launch-libraries4blacklives/.

38. "Librariesrespond" hashtag, Twitter, twitter.com/hashtag/librariesrespond.

39. Jody Gray and John Amundsen, "Libraries Respond to Recent Crises," American Libraries Magazine (blog), July 11, 2016, americanlibrariesmagazine.org/blogs/the-scoop/libraries-respond-recent-crises/.

40. Ibid.

41. twitter.com/hashtag/liulockout.

42. Scott Jaschik, "LIU Faculty Lockout Ends," *Inside Higher Ed* (September 2016), www.insidehighered.com/news/2016/09/15/union-announces-end-faculty-lockout-long-island-u.

43. Ibid.

44. Critlib.org, "#LIUlockout," accessed November 21, 2016, critlib.org/liulockout-chat/.

45. https://twitter.com/hashtag/weneeddiversebooks.

46. We Need Diverse Books, "FAQ," accessed November 21, 2016, weneeddiversebooks.org/faq/.

47. We Need Diverse Books, "Mission Statement," accessed November 21, 2016, weneeddiversebooks.org/mission-statement/.

48. twitter.com/hashtag/ownvoices.

49. Corinne Duyvis, "#ownvoices," accessed November 21, 2016, www.corinneduyvis.net/ownvoices/.

50. bell hooks, *Teaching to Transgress* (New York: Routledge, 1994), 14, 59–75.

BIBLIOGRAPHY

American Library Association. "Core Values of Librarianship." Accessed November 21, 2016. www.ala.org/advocacy/intfreedom/statementspols/corevalues.

———. "Diversity Counts 2009–2010 Update." Accessed November 21, 2016. www.ala.org/offices/diversity/diversitycounts/2009-2010update.

Anantachai, Tarida, Latrice Booker, Althea Lazzaro, and Martha Parker. "Establishing a Communal Network for Professional Advancement among Librarians of Color." In *Where Are All the Librarians of Color?*, edited by Rebecca Hankins and Miguel Juárez, 31–53. Sacramento: Library Juice Press, 2015.

Bourg, Chris. "Libraries, Technology, and Social Justice." The Feral Librarian (blog). October 7, 2016. chrisbourg.wordpress.com/2016/10/07/libraries-technology-and-social-justice/.

Chan, Emily K., Jovanni Lota, Holly A. Smith, and Steven D. Booth. "Discovering Librarianship: Personalizing the Recruitment Process for Under-Represented Students." In *Where Are All the Librarians of Color?*, edited by Rebecca Hankins and Miguel Juárez, 11–30. Sacramento: Library Juice Press, 2015.

Cox, Ernie J. "Twitter for All: Expanding Professional Dialogue with Social Media." *Library Media Connection* 28, no. 5 (2010): 52–53.

Critlib.org. "About/Join the Discussion." Accessed November 21, 2016. critlib.org/about/.

———. "Critiquing #critlib." Accessed November 21, 2016. critlib.org/critiquing-critlib/.

———. "Feelings." Accessed November 21, 2016. critlib.org/feelings/.

———. "Library Workers with Disabilities." Accessed January 9, 2017. critlib.org/library-workers-with-disabilities/.

———. "#LIUlockout." Accessed November 21, 2016. critlib.org/liulockout-chat/.

Critlib Unconference 2015. "About." Accessed November 21, 2016. critlib2015.weebly.com/.

Dutton Ewbanks, Ann. "Library Advocacy through Twitter: A Social Media Analysis of #savelibraries and #getESEAright." *School Libraries Worldwide* 21, no. 2 (2015): 26–38.

Duyvis, Corinne. "#ownvoices." Accessed November 21, 2016. www.corinneduyvis.net/ownvoices/.

Eckert, Cory. "Opinion: Libraries Are Not Neutral." *School Library Journal*. August 2016. www.slj.com/2016/08/opinion/libraries-are-not-neutral-opinion/.

The FANG Collective. "#NoDAPL Solidarity." Accessed November 21, 2016. nodaplsolidarity.org/.

Fox, Violet. Twitter post. December 6, 2016. twitter.com/violetbfox/status/806329606383038464.

Gray, Jody, and John Amundsen. "Libraries Respond to Recent Crises." American Libraries Magazine (blog). July 11, 2016. americanlibrariesmagazine.org/blogs/the-scoop/libraries-respond-recent-crises/.

Hathcock, April M. "DO THE WORK!!! #libleadgender Chat March 9." At the Intersection (blog). March 4, 2016. aprilhathcock.wordpress.com/2016/03/04/do-the-work-libleadgender-chat-march-9.

hooks, bell. *Teaching to Transgress*. New York: Routledge, 1994.

Jaschik, Scott. "LIU Faculty Lockout Ends." *Inside Higher Ed*. September 2016. www.insidehighered.com/news/2016/09/15/union-announces-end-faculty-lockout-long-island-u.

Jules, Bergis. "Documenting the Now Project." Presentation at the Collections as Data: Stewardship and Use Models to Enhance Access symposium at the Library of Congress, Washington, D.C., September 27, 2016.

Kooy, Brian K. "Building Virtually Free Subject Area Expertise through Social Media: An Exploratory Study." *College & Research Libraries* 77, no. 4 (2016): 423–54.

Leach, Erin. Twitter post. September 9, 2016. twitter.com/erinaleach/status/774257721596 051457.

Lee, Maria R., David C. Yen, and C. Y. Hsiao. "Understanding the Perceived Community Value of Facebook Users." *Computers in Human Behavior* 35 (June 2014): 350–58.

Libraries 4 Black Lives. "Take the Pledge." Accessed November 21, 2016. libraries4blacklives .org/pledge/.

———. Twitter post. August 8, 2016. twitter.com/Libs4BlackLives/status/76274002793988 0960.

———. "Your Ideas." Accessed November 21, 2016. libraries4blacklives.org/yourideas/.

Mccracken, Krista. Twitter post. December 14, 2016. twitter.com/kristamccracken/sta tus/809205692968161280.

McLean, Jessica, Sophia Maalsen, and Alana Grech. "Learning about Feminism in Digital Spaces: Online Methodologies and Participatory Mapping." *Australian Geographer* 47, no. 2 (2016): 157–77.

Meeks, Amanda. Twitter post. December 14, 2016. twitter.com/A_meeksie/status/8092044 50053062656.

Mountz, Alison et al. "For Slow Scholarship: A Feminist Politics of Resistance through Collective Action in the Neoliberal University." *ACME: An International E-Journal for Critical Geographies* 14, no. 4 (2015): 1235–59.

Olin, Jessica. "#libleadgender and Self-Care." Storify (chat). October 5, 2016. storify.com/ olinj/libleadgender-and-self-care.

Olin, Jessica, and Michelle Millet. "Gendered Expectations for Leadership in Libraries." In the Library with the Lead Pipe. November 2015. www.inthelibrarywiththeleadpipe.org/2015/ libleadgender/.

Peet, Lisa. "Public Librarians Launch Libraries4BlackLives." *Library Journal.* August 2016. lj.libraryjournal.com/2016/08/people/public-librarians-launch-libraries4blacklives/#.

Roberts, Sarah T., and Safiya Umoja Noble. "Empowered to Name, Inspired to Act: Social Responsibility and Diversity as Calls to Action in the LIS Context." *Library Trends* 64, no. 3 (2016): 512–32.

Schomberg, Jessica. Twitter post. December 6, 2016. twitter.com/schomj/status/8063289 02641709056.

Statista. "Number of Monthly Active Twitter Users Worldwide from 1st Quarter 2010 to 3rd Quarter 2016 (in Millions)." Accessed November 21, 2016. www.statista.com/statis tics/282087/number-of-monthly-active-twitter-users/.

Tewell, Eamon. "Putting Critical Information Literacy into Context: How and Why Librarians Adopt Critical Practices in Their Teaching." In the Library with the Lead Pipe. October 2016. www.inthelibrarywiththeleadpipe.org/2016/putting-critical-information-literacy into-context-how-and-why-librarians-adopt-critical-practices-in-their-teaching/.

We Need Diverse Books. "FAQ." Accessed November 21, 2016. weneeddiversebooks.org/faq/.

———. "Mission Statement." Accessed November 21, 2016. weneeddiversebooks.org/ mission-statement/.

Young, Scott W. H., and Doralyn Rossmann. "Building Library Community through Social Media." *Information Technology and Libraries* 34, no. 1 (2015): 20–37.

Index

About the Editors and Contributors

EDITORS

Scott W. H. Young is an assistant professor and digital initiatives librarian at Montana State University Library. He has published and presented on user experience, participatory design, social media, and web privacy. Young and Rossmann recently designed and delivered a new credited course for undergraduate students at Montana State, entitled Contemporary Approaches to Community Building Using Social Media. Young earned an MLIS from Long Island University and an MA in archives and public history from New York University. On Twitter, he can be found at @hei_scott.

Doralyn Rossmann is an associate professor, administrative director of Data Infrastructure and Scholarly Communication (DISC), and head of Collection Development at Montana State University Library. Her recent research includes presentations and publications in public budgeting, library-vendor relations, and social media including ethics, optimization, and community building. Rossmann has an MSLS and a BA in political science and English from the University of North Carolina–Chapel Hill and a master's in public administration from Montana State University. Rossmann and Young recently co-authored a Library Technology Report from the American Library Association, "Social Media Optimization: Principles for Building and Engaging Community." On Twitter, she can be found at @doralyn.

CONTRIBUTORS

Katie Elson Anderson is a reference and instruction librarian at Paul Robeson Library, Rutgers University–Camden. Anderson is the liaison to the Business, Psychology and Anthropology, and Sociology and Criminal Justice Departments. Her research focuses on social media, Internet culture, online communities, and digital storytelling. She studies these topics as they relate to libraries, as well as their impact and implications on society. Her participatory research on these topics gives her many opportunities to learn, explore, and connect with others who share the same interests, an added bonus to the research.

Lisa Bunker has been managing social media for Pima County Public Library since 2009 and teaches social media to Tucson-area businesses and non-profits. Lisa was recognized in 2012 as a Library Journal Mover and Shaker, an international award for people who help move libraries forward in the twenty-first century.

Christopher Chan is head of Information Services at the Hong Kong Baptist University Library, where he is responsible for instruction and reference services. His research interests include information literacy assessment and the use of social media to promote library services, with his work appearing in *Reference Services Review*, *Library Management*, and *Communications in Information Literacy*, among others. He obtained his MLIS from Charles Sturt University and also holds a master of education from the University of Hong Kong.

Patricia J. Devine is the outreach and communications coordinator for the National Network of Libraries of Medicine, Pacific NW Region in Seattle, where she designs and implements outreach programs for health-care providers and librarians. Her research interests include social determinants of health, health disparities, and using social media to reach underserved populations. She obtained her BA from Evergreen State College and her MLS from the University of Washington.

Jarrett M. Drake is a PhD student in cultural anthropology at Harvard University and an advisory archivist for A People's Archives of Police Violence in Cleveland. His lines of inquiry converge on issues of justice, state violence, accountability, and memory work. Prior to Harvard, Jarrett was the digital archivist at the Princeton University Archives. Jarrett earned a BA in history from Yale College and an MSI (archives and records management) from the University of Michigan School of Information.

Stony Evans is a school library media specialist at Lakeside High School in Hot Springs, Arkansas. He earned his MS in library media and information technologies from the University of Central Arkansas. He is a member of ALA and AASL. Stony has written several articles for *School Library Connection* magazine.

Angel M. Gondek currently serves as a branch manager in the Columbus Metropolitan Library system. Prior to her current position, Angel was the circulation supervisor at Columbus State Community College. She holds a dual BA in English and linguistics from The Ohio State University and an MLIS from Kent State University.

Joanna Hare is a subject librarian at City University of Hong Kong, where she supports five diverse faculties in teaching, learning, and research. She is also the manager of the library's social media presence and coordinator of the Media Resources Collection. In this last role, she represents CityU Library on the Joint University Librarians Advisory Committee (JULAC) Committee on Media. Her professional and research interests include teaching and research support for humanities and the arts, information and digital literacy, and innovative approaches to customer service. Joanna holds a bachelor's in media from Macquarie University and an MA in information management from RMIT University.

April M. Hathcock is the scholarly communication librarian at New York University in New York City. Her research interests include diversity and inclusion in librarianship, cultural creation and exchange, and the ways in which social and legal infrastructures benefit the works of certain groups over others. She is the author of the article "White Librarianship in Blackface: Diversity Initiatives in LIS" and the blog At the Intersection, which examines issues at the intersection of feminism, libraries, social justice, and the law. On Twitter, she can be found at the handle @AprilHathcock.

Dana A. Knott is library coordinator at Columbus State Community College's Delaware (Ohio) Campus Learning Center. She currently serves as the Academic Library Association of Ohio's Instruction Interest Group Co-Chair. Library-related articles and creative works have appeared in *College & Research Libraries News*, *Bitter Oleander*, *Emrys Journal*, and *Karamu*. Dana holds an MLIS and an MA in English.

Laura Little is an instructional designer and adjunct instructor at Connecticut College, where she also manages the Language and Culture Center. Laura received a BA in Russian and French from the University of Missouri at Columbia and an MA in Slavic studies from the University of Wisconsin–Madison. A teacher and scholar by training, she has taught at and developed curricula for Beloit College, Middlebury College, and the Defense Language Institute. At Connecticut College, she works with a broad array of instructional technologies, striving in all her roles to meaningfully integrate digital tools and material culture into curricula.

Andrew Lopez is a research support and instruction librarian at Connecticut College, where he coordinates the library's role in the Federal Depository Library Program (FDLP). He serves on the Africana Studies Steering Committee, which aims to revitalize the Africana Studies major at the college, as well as the Dean's Conduct

Committee, which resolves violations of the Honor Code. Outside of work, he is active in nearby neighborhood organizations that often work with college classes on community partnerships. He has an MLIS from McGill University and a BA in philosophy and French from Temple University.

Jessica McCullough is an instructional design librarian at Connecticut College. She designs programming for faculty on the intentional integration of technology to achieve learning goals for all students. She received an MSI from the School of Information, University of Michigan and an MA in educational technology from George Washington University.

Rebecca Parmer is the college archivist at Connecticut College. She received an MS in archival management from Simmons College and a BA in English from Scripps College. Previously, she worked for the USS *Constitution* Museum and Northeastern University. Her professional research interests include archival pedagogy, undergraduate education, and inquiry-based engagement in college and university archives.